D0617430

Lebenthal On Munis

Lebenthal On Munis

**Straight Talk
About Tax-Free Municipal Bonds
for the Troubled Investor Deciding,
"Yes ..." or "No!"**

New York

Lebenthal On Munis

Straight Talk About Tax-Free Municipal Bonds
for the Troubled Investor Deciding, "Yes… or No!"

Copyright © 2009 Jim Lebenthal. All rights reserved.

No part of this publication may be reproduced or transmitted in any form or by any means, mechanical or electronic, including photocopying and recording, or by any information storage and retrieval system, without permission in writing from the author or publisher (except by a reviewer, who may quote brief passages and/or short brief video clips in a review.)

Disclaimer: The Publisher and the Author make no representations or warranties with respect to the accuracy or completeness of the contents of this work and specifically disclaim all warranties, including without limitation warranties of fitness for a particular purpose. No warranty may be created or extended by sales or promotional materials. The advice and strategies contained herein may not be suitable for every situation. This work is sold with the understanding that the Publisher is not engaged in rendering legal, accounting, or other professional services. If professional assistance is required, the services of a competent professional person should be sought. Neither the Publisher nor the Author shall be liable for damages arising herefrom. The fact that an organization or website is referred to in this work as a citation and/or a potential source of further information does not mean that the Author or the Publisher endorses the information the organization or website may provide or recommendations it may make. Further, readers should be aware that internet websites listed in this work may have changed or disappeared between when this work was written and when it is read.

ISBN 978-1-60037-656-6

Library of Congress Control Number:

MORGAN · JAMES
THE ENTREPRENEURIAL PUBLISHER

Morgan James Publishing, LLC
1225 Franklin Ave., STE 325
Garden City, NY 11530-1693
Toll Free 800-485-4943
www.MorganJamesPublishing.com

Habitat
for Humanity®
Peninsula
Building Partner

In an effort to support local communities, raise awareness and funds, Morgan James Publishing donates one percent of all book sales for the life of each book to Habitat for Humanity. Get involved today, visit **www.HelpHabitatForHumanity.org**.

Contents

Preface

Because Disclosure Isn't an Option. It's the Law.

I WAS BORN just one year before
the crash. My father and mother were
the husband-and-wife team of Louis and
Sayra Lebenthal, founders of Lebenthal
& Company, Municipal Bonds for the
Individual Investor. I remember an almanac
Dad first compiled in the thirties and kept
up-to-date with woodcuts of tornados and
natural disasters through which municipal
bonds had kept right on paying.

Those icons of the safety record of
municipal bonds in the face of calamity—
the great Chicago Fire, the San Francisco
earthquake, the Galveston hurricane

*Despite the National Industrial
Recovery Act being struck down by the
Supreme Court, its Blue Eagle sticker
is still remembered by survivors of the
Great Depression.*

connect me to rough times municipal bonds have weathered, past and present.
I'm thinking of visits to Lebenthal & Company with the Depression in full swing.
I can still see beaten men in fedoras selling apples out on the street downstairs …
while upstairs in our window on the fourteenth floor, our National (Industrial)
Recovery Administration (NRA) Blue Eagle window sticker proudly proclaimed
to one and all—from the fourteenth floor yet—"We Do Our Part."

THE RECORD OF MUNICIPAL BONDS IN THE FACE OF LOCAL CALAMITIES EMPHASIZES THEIR SAFETY

FIRE

From October 8th to October 11th, in 1871, the Great Fire raged in the City of Chicago. Losses were estimated at $196,000,000. Eighteen thousand buildings were destroyed. Both principal and interest on Chicago's bonds were paid in full. . . . On November 9th, 1872, Boston, Massachusetts, experienced a conflagration which destroyed 748 buildings. Both principal and interest on Boston's bonds were paid in full. . . . On February 7th, 1904, Baltimore, Md., experienced a great fire in which 2500 buildings were destroyed. Principal and interest on Baltimore's bonds were paid in full.

EARTHQUAKE

On August 31st, 1886, Charleston, South Carolina, was prostrated with an earthquake. Both principal and interest on Charleston's bonds were paid in full. . . . On April 18th and 19th, the San Francisco earthquake and accompanying fire took over 500 lives and caused property loss amounting to $400,000,000. Both principal and interest on San Francisco's bonds were paid in full.

FLOOD

On March 25th, 26th and 27th, 1913, floods occurred in Ohio and Indiana which took 732 lives and caused great property damage. At the same time floods in Brazos, Texas, took 500 lives and caused terrific damage. Both principal and interest on the bonds of all the communities affected by these floods were paid in full. . . . On July 3rd and 4th, 1921, Arkansas River floods and rain at Pueblo, Colorado, made 3500 persons homeless and caused the death of 1500 people with property losses of $20,000,000. Principal and interest on Pueblo's bonds were paid in full.

TORNADO

On May 17th, 1896, a tornado at St. Louis killed several hundred people and caused great property damage. Both principal and interest on St. Louis' bonds were paid in full. . . . On September 8th, 1900, the Galveston, Texas, tornado took 6000 lives and caused tremendous property damage. This is the only case in more than 60 years wherein bond holders had to take a loss of interest. For five years Galveston paid interest totaling 50% of that due, and thereafter paid interest in full. The principal was never affected.

EXPLOSION

On April 16, 1947, a nitrate-laden French freighter exploded in the Gulf of Mexico off Texas City, Texas. 512 persons were killed, with total property damage amounting to $50,000,000. Bondholders were unaffected. . . . On May 19, 1950, 600 tons of ammunition exploded in the bay off South Amboy, N. J. The explosion broke windows and shook houses over a 40-mile radius. According to the New York Times 29 people were killed, more than 400 injured and the city of 8000 was wrecked. There was no interruption of interest or principal payments on South Amboy's bonds.

19   LEBENTHAL & CO., NEW YORK

An exciting first impression of municipal bonds from a vintage Lebenthal & Company brochure.

It was a scene out of that Edward Hopper painting, *Office at Night*. There was our Miss Dodd, bookkeeper-stenographer-telephone operator, plugging in calls at the switchboard. Dad clutching the upright telephone in one hand, the receiver up to his ear in the other … the office goldfish surfing the fish tank for something to eat … me, for pre-TV fun and excitement, linking paper clips together in an endless chain, which the "customers men," to their grief, would not discover until the next time they reached for a paper clip … or filling paper cups of water just to watch bubbles glug-glug up the water cooler jug. Closing time Saturdays was 3 o'clock. Dad would cover the canary cage, push the elevator button, and as we left, say, "Good night!" to the elevator man. That bothered me. "Dad, it's still afternoon. Why are we saying good night?" "Oh, son!" Dad exclaimed.

That I should ever end up in such an office scene was out of the question. So, after graduating Princeton, I took the glamour road with dream jobs at *Life* magazine, NBC, Disney, Young & Rubicam Advertising, and Ogilvy & Mather. (For more about fifteen years and tons of fun working for Henry Luce, Walt Disney, and David Ogilvy, while avoiding the family bond business, read *Confessions of a Municipal Bond Salesman,* John Wiley & Sons, Inc., publisher.) Guilt finally got me pondering, *What am I doing here? Why was I making other companies famous instead of putting my family's name on every tongue and building an empire for Lebenthal?* Ever since Dad's death in 1951, Mother kept the company going, barely hiding the hope that one day, I'd … Well, let's just say that when I finally did cave in and join her selling "odd-lot" municipal bonds to the little guy with a thousand dollars or so to invest at a time, she let it out: "At last you've gotten all that other foolishness out of your system."

That was way back in heady 1963, before landlords in the South Bronx started walking away from buildings that were worth less than the bills for back taxes. It was before New York City began borrowing for daily operating expenses. It was before the City declared a "moratorium" (you can pronounce it "default") on the repayment of $1.6 billion municipal notes, and before the flag touched the ground in Washington, Oregon, and Idaho, the home states of the Washington Public Power Supply System (WPPSS).

My formal education in tax-free municipal bonds began long before inroads were made on their hallowed exclusion from income tax, before the Social Security tax, before the alternative minimum tax on certain municipal bonds deemed "private activity bonds," and before the outright ban of tax-exempt bonds for ballparks, convention centers, liquor stores, and private jets. Municipal bonds still had twenty-five glorious years to go before the Supreme Court would knock tax exemption off its constitutional high horse and rule in *South Carolina v. Baker* that municipal bonds were tax free only by the grace of Congress, not by any constitutional right.

I sat at a desk across from my mother's and got on-the-job-training from the master. Today, I *own* the verities "my momma done told me."

It's not how much you earn that counts. It's how much you keep.

If you're going to speculate, don't do it in municipal bonds.

Municipal bonds are for tax-free income, not to make a killing from market moves.

A good portfolio diversifies maturities as well as municipalities.

If you know you're going to need your money in two, five, ten years, buy bonds that mature in two, five, ten years. Why subject your savings to the vagaries of the market?

A bond is marketable when you can get a bid on it before maturity from other firms and not just the house you bought it from.

The best time to invest in munis is whenever you have the funds.

If it's knowable, make sure the customer knows it. If it isn't, don't pretend.

Besides "listen to your mother," I believe in taking on, taking over, and making whatever you do your own. And, true to form, here I go now making a certain rule of the game my own, as if I were the one who thought it up and not the regulators:

"A broker has a duty to disclose all material information in connection with an investment recommendation ... which may be reasonably relevant to an investor to take into consideration in making an informed investment decision ... in particular the various risks and level of risk of an investment recommendation."

—THE NASD (NOW FINRA)
OBLIGATION OF DISCLOSURE RULE

Giving you enough information to decide whether you really belong in municipal bonds—and which ones—isn't a choice that's up to me to make. It's the law. And *Lebenthal on Munis* is going to toughen that law by giving you the information to decide "No!" as well as "Yes," even if it means turning me and my bonds thumbs down.

Am I afraid that disclosing the *why nots*, as well as the *whys*, will kill the sale? I hope only the unsuitable sales that weren't meant to happen. After all, I am a municipal bond salesman, living by the best money-making claim Lebenthal & Company has advertised in all its eighty-plus-year history: "disclosing the risks about municipal bonds, and helping investors decide, 'Yes ...' or 'No!'"

1

"Second in Safety Only to U.S. Treasuries, Son." Verily! Verily!

IN THE YEAR 1963, when sowing oats for me ceased at age thirty-five and seeking happiness and self-fulfillment in municipal bonds began, 75 percent of the new munis coming to market were so-called full faith and credit, unlimited tax general obligation bonds (GOs), considered the blue chips of the bond business.

GOs are backed by *all* the revenue generating powers of the municipality—the main one being the power of the issuer to peg real-property taxes at whatever rate it takes to pay the interest it owes and principal at maturity. For a GO, payment of debt service isn't an option. It's a must. And bondholders have *prior lien* on the property tax, meaning bondholders get paid ahead of everyone else. Theoretically they do. Prior lien could turn out to be academic if the money to pay just plain isn't there. Yet just the existence of prior lien in Article VIII, Section 2 of the State of New York Constitution inspired me in 1975 to run a full-page ad in the *New York Times* that laid it on the line: "As a New York City bondholder, you get yours, before policemen, before firemen, before school teachers, even before the mayor." By the end of the year, New York City declared the moratorium and reneged on $1.6 billion general obligation municipal notes.

THE NEW YORK TIMES, FRIDAY, APRIL 4, 1975

The Second Safest Investment In America.

The greatest threat to New York City is not a loss of cash flow.

It's a loss of confidence.

Standard & Poor's only added to that threat Wednesday by continuing to undermine investor confidence when they suspended their rating on New York City bonds.

It's about time somebody in the financial community spoke up for the city. So Lebenthal is going on record publicly with this ad.

We've been selling New York City bonds for over 49 years, and we intend to continue. Because to us, the bonds still deserve that confidence. And we judge them by some pretty tough standards.

First of all, we believe in them because they are general obligation bonds. And general obligation bonds are regarded by financial experts as second in safety only to U.S. Government bonds.

The reason is they're backed by unlimited taxes on real estate and by any other tax a city levies. Under the Constitution of the State of New York, real estate taxes must be pegged at whatever rate it takes to pay off the bonds.

Even when real estate taxes go up and reach a point of diminishing returns, the bonds are safe. Because paying bondholders has priority over all other municipal obligations.

Under Article VIII, Section 2 of the State Constitution, the owner of the General Obligation of any town in New York State has first lien on every penny in that issuer's treasury, regardless of what else that money might have been tagged for.

Bondholders must be paid by law. Before the policemen. Before firemen. Before welfare recipients. Even before the mayor.

But even with all these legal safeguards, you might still worry about how safe your bonds would be in a real crisis.

One way to answer that fear is to look at what happened during one of the biggest crises in this country's history: The Great Depression.

As a class, general obligation bonds performed quite well. The most coupon interest and bond principal that was a month or more late at any one time was $320 million. Or 1.7% of the debt outstanding.

In virtually every case, however, bondholders received payment in full. And while 48 municipalities with populations over 25,000 had some difficulty and were late paying during the Depression, New York City was not one of them.

In fact, through two depressions, five wars, and any number of recessions, New York's payment record has been absolutely flawless.

For all these reasons, we still say general obligation bonds—including New York City's—are the second safest investment in America—second only to U.S. Government bonds.

Which would make losing confidence in New York second only to losing confidence in America.

We want to be your Heroes.

How Lebenthal & Company sought to reassure investors about the safety of New York City general obligation bonds in the city's 1975 fiscal crisis. Not so fast, said the SEC.

2

That ad grabbed more than just the public's eye. It also caught the attention of the SEC. So that when the SEC conducted its investigation into the mass marketing of New York City bonds to the man in the street, it earned me eight anguished hours on the hot seat (with an hour off for lunch) defending the audacity of putting prior lien into layman's language. "Where'd you get this stuff?" the investigator doing the grilling asked. "Where? Bond lore, sir, learned at the breast."

It was a beautiful day for me when the highest court in the state quashed the moratorium and told the city it had to pay up, adding, "a general obligation is not only an obligation to pay from available revenues, but an obligation to generate the revenues to pay." So yes, when a town is having difficulties balancing the budget, debt service isn't the last thing on the issuer's list of bills to be paid. Prior lien means it's the first. With that off my chest, now let me get practical.

Asbury Park, New Jersey, was flat broke, its taxing power exhausted, and it defaulted in the Depression. In 1942, the Supreme Court of the United States upheld a plan that refunded Asbury Park's defaulted bonds with longer maturities at full face value, but at a lower rate of interest. Justice Felix Frankfurter gave the opinion in Faitoute Iron & Steel Co. v. City of Asbury Park, N.J. "The notion that a city has unlimited taxing power is, of course, an illusion. A city cannot be taken over and operated for the benefit of its creditors." Obviously, all the revenues of a town would not be consumed in debt service, leaving nothing—zero—for the cost of essential services. Kids have to go to school. The garbage has to be hauled. The fire engines have to come. So, police power, public health and safety, and laws of practicality could work against your immediate interest as a bondholder. But they rarely have.

Yes, as a class, a municipal bond backed by the full faith, credit, and taxing power of a city or state comes as close to the absolute as you can hope to get on paper. But "safe," "safety," "guaranteed," only address creditworthiness, the assurance of receiving your interest payments right along and getting your principal back at the end, if you stay the course. If you sell before maturity, you can make money or lose money. It all depends whether interest rates are higher or lower than when you bought your bond and on the fortunes of your particular issuer. Fluctuating resale values are simply a fact of life. Bonds go up. Bonds go down. "Market risk" goes with the territory. "Credit risk" is something else. Chancing not getting paid for a yield that is too good to be true is looking for trouble, unless of course, you know what you're doing, you're doing it with play money, and are out to pick up someone else's heartache for pennies on the dollar. Dad, who knew what he was doing, did it with bonds for draining the Florida Everglades in the forties. Those bonds still drained more out of him than they ever did the Everglades.

When uncertainty reigns, and the flight to safety is on, Treasuries and munis are ports in the storm. A comforting statistic has worked its way deeper and deeper into municipal bond lore: permanent loss of interest and principal from recorded defaults during the 1929–1937 Depression period totaled $100 million, a mere one-half of 1 percent of the average amount of state and local debt outstanding.

I grew up living with that one-half of 1 percent figure as an article of faith, until the day I discovered the rest of the story in a thin but loaded study of municipal bond defaults in *The Postwar Quality of State and Local Debt* by George H. Hempel. According to Hempel, 15 percent of the average amount of municipal debt outstanding—$2.85 billion, representing 4,771 state and local units—paid late and were in temporary default at one time or another in the 1929–1937 period. So, where did municipals get that sterling reputation for safety? From their record for eventual repayment. In the 1930s, almost all municipal bonds were GOs, obligated by law to pay. Default isn't allowed. There's also a practical reason why our towns will break their necks to make good, even when the chips are down. To default could permanently damage an issuer's credit. And without credit, the cash-flow problems, the budget problems, and all the other problems that existed before default become worse. Default only postpones the inevitable obligation to pay the full amount due.

Lateness does not forgive indebtedness. But I do want to acknowledge the legal out that could undo your hold on the issuer: Chapter 9 of the Federal Bankruptcy Law, as amended. Under the previous law, holders of 51 percent of an issuer's debt had to consent to any plan that involved taking less than 100 cents on the dollar, before a court would even entertain the plan. Consent of the debt holder for the purpose of getting into court is done away with under the amended Chapter 9. Now a municipality can get into court and obtain Chapter 9 relief, if it is insolvent, has permission from the state to file for bankruptcy, has a plan to adjust its debts, and satisfies other conditions among them:

- the plan has the consent of the holders of at least a majority of the issuer's debt that would be adversely affected,

- the bankrupt has negotiated in good faith but failed to reach agreement, or

- negotiating is totally impractical.

Lateness, by itself, is not bankruptcy. Bankruptcy has to be a formal proceeding in federal court, because the Constitution of the United States forbids the states on their own to pass laws impairing the obligations of contracts. Unless a town throws in the towel and files the petition in federal bankruptcy court that it is unable to meet its obligation, the obligation to pay in full remains in force.

By Hempel's lights, of the 48 cities with populations over 25,000 that were in default all were reported out of the hole by 1938. Such are the legal and pragmatic obligations to pay that among those forty-eight defaulting cities, five solved their defaults without any change of contract, twenty-eight did not scale down interest or principal in their refunding operations, fifteen scaled interest only, and no city in this group had any reduction of principal.

As an investor considering municipal bonds and knowing the one-half of 1 percent permanent loss but 15 percent late payment record, how would you react to a replay of the Depression scenario? Past performance is no guarantee of future results, but it does tell you what the insurance companies were thinking when they weighed the pros and cons of taking on the risk of guaranteeing the payment of municipal bonds. There may be a model here for informing your own investment decision.

Think about it. Insuring a municipal bond is the same bet on its *not* defaulting that you make when you buy a bond. It was the minuscule one-half of 1 percent permanent default figure that convinced the insurance companies this business of guaranteeing municipal bonds would be carrying the proverbial coals to Newcastle. For one thing, being late does not accelerate payment of interest and principal before it actually comes due. And by the time the full amount does become due, the Depression showed that the municipality would have the time to get back on its feet and cure the deficiency. Municipalities don't need bond insurance other than for marketing reasons and to lower borrowing costs by coming to market "triple-A, insured." What a peach of a business! It was when the municipal bond insurance companies took to wrapping with their guarantee and good name pools of subprime mortgages, packaged into Collateralized Debt Obligations (CDOs), already inexplicably deemed triple-A by the rating agencies, that the insurers then became casualties of the subprime mortgage disaster.

In 2005, the heyday of municipal bond insurance, 56 percent of the $408 billion new bonds that came to market were insured and rated triple-A by Fitch, Moody's, and Standard & Poor's. Ninety-eight percent of the 56 percent were guaranteed as to payment by the original big four insurers—AMBAC, FGIC, FSA, and MBIA. Since being stripped of their triple-A ratings, bonds insured by AMBAC, FGIC, and MBIA currently trade in the open market based on the rating of the underlying bonds, as if they had no insurance at all. Just when local economies are being strained by hard times, the value of municipal bond insurance is unquantifiable—and won't be known until an insured bond defaults and the guarantee is put to the test. Who wants to be stuck with an insured bond until that happens and find out the hard way what the insurance is worth? Stay tuned for an answer from FGIC-insured Jefferson County, Alabama—county seat, Birmingham.

Jefferson County debt is already past due on $3.2 billion sewer bonds that would be in default but for the forbearance of creditors who have agreed to stand still insofar as pressing their claim. Jefferson County is on the brink of filing for bankruptcy. What a feat it would be for all the municipal bond insurance companies if FGIC, once AAA, then CCC, and now unrated, had to make good on its guarantee—and actually could! Or, if an industry-wide consortium of municipal bond insurers stepped up to the plate and reinsured the troubled bonds. That kind of joint effort might save the day for the municipal bond insurance industry, while preventing the largest default in municipal bond history.

In the entire decade of the 1990s, according to Standard & Poor's, less than 1 percent of the average municipal bonds of all types outstanding were late paying. A surprisingly large number of $827 million out of $9.83 billion defaults were general obligation bonds, owing to one single issuer: bankrupt Orange County and its default on $800 million school GOs. After a year, when Orange County got back on track and repaid the $800 million, total GO defaults dropped down to $27 million, in the scheme of things almost zero. Until confidence in municipal bond insurance is restored, it's back to asking the kind of questions you almost forgot to ask, when most of the bonds that came to market were triple-A insured. You now have to analyze an underlying bond with insurance on the borrower's own ability to pay, its insurance be hanged.

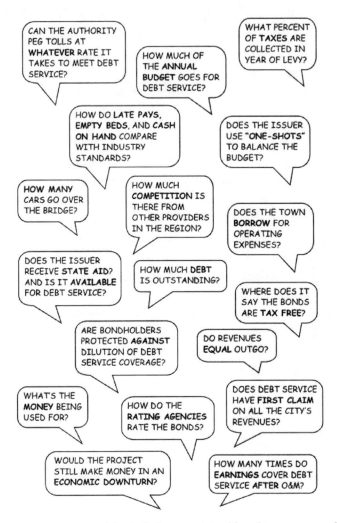

Oh the things investors would ask, before municipal bond insurance and so many AAAs suspended critical judgment.

So far, the power behind the GO to tax and the power behind the revenue bond to charge for a necessity of life have kept the flag off the ground. But, suffice to say, bad times don't just float up there in the clouds. It rains on the same place where the sun shines and where the revenues have to come from in all seasons—the cities and towns where the people, their homes, jobs, factories, and farms are. Advice to the trusting as well as the suspicious and questioning: go into municipals with your Hempels and your eyes open.

2

Income, and No Tax:
How Long Can a Good Thing Last?

SINCE 1913, EVERY federal income tax law has exempted municipal bond income from federal income tax, although with increasing restrictions and limitations. When a state, U.S. territory, or local government needs money to build, say, a new sewage disposal facility, it borrows it in the tax-free municipal bond market—from firms like mine. We, in turn, lay off the loan, $25,000 here, $100,000 there, to investors like you (for a profit, known as the "takedown," averaging $5 per thousand face value). Two beneficiaries and one interested onlooker are involved.

Beneficiary One: The issuer who is able to borrow at below market rates because of the demand for any income that is tax free.

Beneficiary Two: You, the lender, who take a lower rate of return, hoping to gain more in taxes saved than in interest forgone.

The Interested Onlooker is the IRS, watching and almost tasting the mouth-watering aroma of $72.9 billion (in the year 2006 alone) in untaxable municipal bond interest waft under its nose like a pie cooling on a windowsill.

At first, immunity from taxation was accepted constitutional doctrine. The states couldn't destroy the instruments of the federal government for carrying on its lawful affairs. And the Feds couldn't tax the bonds of the states and their political subdivisions. But then in South Carolina v. Baker, 1988, the Supreme Court struck down a century of established case law with these words to the wise: "States must find their protection from Congressional regulation through the national political process," and not look to the Constitution. Oh, munis are still tax free—but only by the grace of Congress and only as long as 535 senators and representatives are convinced that states and communities should be allowed to borrow at low tax- free interest rates for genuinely needed public works. On the other hand, the case for tax exemption weakens when the spread between tax-free and taxable interest rates narrows to the vanishing point. The tax collector starts licking his lips when the issuer saves too little and the buyer of its bonds pockets too much. Would Congress ever tax municipal bonds? Would they? Could they? They can. And they do with:

- estate taxes on the lower of market value at time of death or six months later

- capital gains or ordinary income taxes on market appreciation

- the Social Security tax on municipal bond interest

- the alternative minimum tax on so-called private activity bonds

- the outright ban of tax-exempt bonds for ballparks, health spas, funding state and municipal pensions, and anything else deemed blatantly nongovernmental

All that, plus rulings allowing the IRS to declare the interest of any municipal bond taxable that has not been issued in compliance with tax law.

One other question periodically pops up. What if the Congress overhauls the income tax system with a flat tax, consumption tax, or value added tax? What if the new system involves taxing all savings income alike, including municipal bonds, or leveling the playing field and extending tax exemption to all savings income alike? Without making too much of the risk of either happening, I do acknowledge the sensitivity of market values to anything that smacks of encroaching on the last bastion of tax exemption around. Having brought it up, I don't see a change in the preferential tax treatment of outstanding municipal bonds in the cards. But the discussion is heat from the kitchen investors have learned to live with. So consider the suitability of tax free municipal bonds for you in your tax bracket under the laws that exist now. Introducing the Taxable Equivalent Yield Table, the municipal bond industry's Rosetta Stone for turning tax exempt income into money that talks.

NET TAXABLE INCOME: BRACKETS WILL BE ADJUSTED ANNUALLY FOR INFLATION		PRESENT FEDERAL TAX RATES 2009*	TO MATCH A FEDERALLY FREE RETURN OF							
Joint Return	Single Return		2.0%	2.5%	3.0%	3.5%	4.0%	4.5%	5.0%	6.0%
			YOU WOULD HAVE TO EARN							
$ 67,901-$137,050	$ 33,951-$ 82,250	25.0%	2.6%	3.3%	4.0%	4.6%	5.3%	6.0%	6.6%	8.0%
$137,051-$208,850	$ 82,251-$171,550	28.0%	2.7%	3.4%	4.1%	4.8%	5.5%	6.2%	6.9%	8.3%
$208,851-$372,950	$171,551-$372,950	33.0%	2.9%	3.7%	4.4%	5.2%	5.9%	6.7%	7.4%	8.9%
$372,951+	$372,951+	35.0%	3.0%	3.8%	4.6%	5.3%	6.1%	6.9%	7.7%	9.0%

*Prepared by Lebenthal & Co. LLC February 2009. Subject to legislative revision.

Do you belong in tax-free municipal Bonds? Are they suitable *economically* for you? Look up your income tax bracket, and find out how much you would have to earn from a taxable investment, so that after tax in your bracket it matches the tax free return of the muni. In this example, marrieds and singles paying tax on an income in the $250,000 range would be in a 33% federal tax bracket. They would have to find a taxable investment paying them 7.4 percent, to match a 5 percent return that's federally tax free. And that doesn't take into account the value of any exemption from state and local taxes. Do you belong in municipal bonds? You decide. Remember, it's not how much you earn that counts. It's how much you keep. How much do you make? What's your tax bracket? It's a heck of a way to start a conversation, but it's the first question I ask.

NET TAXABLE INCOME: BRACKETS WILL BE ADJUSTED ANNUALLY FOR INFLATION		PRESENT COMBINED NYC/NYS/ FED TAX RATE 2009*	TO MATCH A TRIPLE TAX FREE RETURN IN NYC OF							
			2.0%	2.5%	3.0%	3.5%	4.0%	4.5%	5.0%	6.0%
Joint Return	Single Return		YOU WOULD HAVE TO EARN							
$67,901-$137,050	$33,591-$82,250	32.8%	2.9%	3.7%	4.4%	5.2%	5.9%	6.6%	7.4%	8.9%
$137,051-$208,850	$82,251-$171,550	35.5%	3.1%	3.8%	4.6%	5.4%	6.2%	6.9%	7.7%	9.3%
$208,851-$372,950	$171,551-$372,950	40.0%	3.3%	4.1%	5.0%	5.8%	6.6%	7.5%	8.3%	10.0%
$372,951+	$372,951+	41.8%	3.4%	4.2%	5.1%	6.0%	6.8%	7.7%	8.5%	10...

*Prepared by Lebenthal & Co. LLC February 2009. Subject to legislative revision.

Now consider the additional value of exemption from state and local income taxes. For example, in NYC, where I come from, the municipal bond of any issuer in New York State is triple tax free to NYC taxpayers, double tax free to New Yorkers outside of New York City (assuming no alternative minimum tax on private activity bonds is involved). As a consequence, that same taxable income of $250,000 would bump a local taxpayer into a combined NYC, NYS, and federal tax bracket of 40 percent. Suddenly, 5 percent free of NYC, NYS, and federal income tax would become the equivalent of 8.3 percent from a taxable investment. For New Yorkers outside the city, 5 percent double tax free is like earning 8 percent taxable. Most other states also give their local taxpayers a break and exempt local municipal bonds from their own state and any local income tax.

When you use the Rosetta Stone to determine how much a dollar of income that's tax free is worth in your bracket, just make sure you compare apples to apples. It's a little disingenuous of me to be comparing munis to Treasuries all the time, when for you, the choice of a taxable alternative may be single- or double-A rated corporates or preferreds. Even then, rating for rating, maturity for maturity, in the upper-income tax brackets, munis are usually priced to give the comparable taxable alternative a run for the money.

Market Share

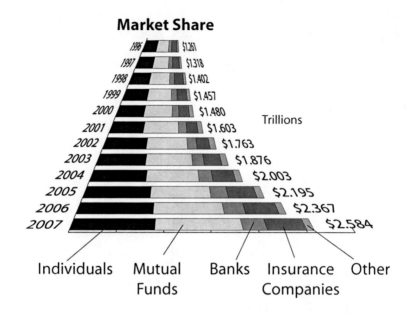

Trillions

1996	$1.261
1997	$1.318
1998	$1.402
1999	$1.457
2000	$1.480
2001	$1.603
2002	$1.763
2003	$1.876
2004	$2.003
2005	$2.195
2006	$2.367
2007	$2.584

Individuals   Mutual   Banks   Insurance   Other
Funds   Companies

Individuals + Mutual Funds = 71% Market Share

THE GROWING POPULARITY OF MUNICIPAL BONDS.
Individual owners of individual bonds (dark bars) and owners through mutual funds (light bars) representing a steady 71% or so of the total volume of bonds outstanding: $1.261 trillion in 1996 to $2.584 trillion at the beginning of 2008. The latest IRS tally indicates that 6,038,822 individual tax returns reported $72,970,971,000 in tax free income in 2006.

Banks and insurance companies used to be the major buyers of municipal bonds, but no more. Flesh-and-blood people, not corporations, are the mainstay of the municipal bond market. Either through direct ownership of 35 percent of the municipal bonds outstanding or indirectly, another 36 percent through mutual funds, individuals own 71 percent of the long-term bonds outstanding. And not because of any love for the hometown sewer system. You know the attraction. A dollar of tax-free income is worth more than 100 cents on the dollar. It is supermoney, worth whatever your own personal income tax bracket makes it worth. Most states also exempt their own bonds from state and local income taxes too. (Their constitutional right to do so while taxing the interest of out-of-state issues was recently questioned and upheld by the United States Supreme Court in Department of Revenue of Kentucky v. Davis, 2008.)

3

In Pursuit of a Knowable, Quotable Fixed Rate of Return:
Yield to Maturity

A MUNICIPAL BOND is a fixed-income investment. (For the moment, take off the table any discussion of VRDOs, variable rate demand obligations.) Interest rate is fixed. Face value at maturity, or to call, is fixed. Between getting your interest right along and cashing in your bond at the end, you will wind up with the "yield to maturity" you were promised, if you hold it to maturity. Everything is set in stone except, "How much will I lose if I have to sell before maturity?"

A funny thing about fixed-income investors. They never ask, how much can I make? It's always, how much will I lose? All right, you can lose money selling before maturity, and you can make money. It depends on whether interest rates are higher or lower when you sell than they were when you bought your bonds—and on the fortunes of your issuer.

Let's look at a typical twenty-year municipal bond—New York State 6s of 1990—through twenty years of the wildest changes in interest rates I know: 1970–1990. The 6s were issued in 1970 at par (100, or $1,000 on the nose for every $1,000 bond). And in 1990 they matured at par. In between, they went through wage and price controls, stagflation, recession, the great inflation, the highest interest rates in U.S. history, the Volcker era, even the stock market crash of 1987. They were up in resale value as high as $1,110 per thousand and down as low as $640 per thousand, all the while spinning off $60 a year per thousand and, come maturity, returning the lump sum payment of $1,000 for every $1,000 borrowed.

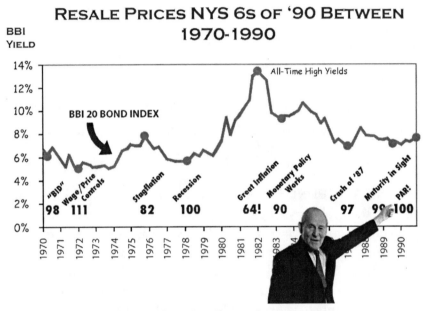

RESALE PRICES NYS 6s OF '90 BETWEEN 1970-1990

In at Par, Out at Par
And What Happened In Between

"How much will I lose if I have to sell?" Here's one answer, using the resale prices New York State 6s of 1990 through the worst period of market volatility I know. They came out at par (100) on June 1, 1970. They matured at par on June 1, 1990. After being up in market value to 111 bid ($1,110 per $1,000), they fell to a low of 64 ($640 per $1,000), when the Bond Buyer 20-Bond Index stood at its all-time inflation high of 13.44 percent. As the Volcker era took hold and maturity approached, so did the magnetic pull of par, the price New York State would be paying to redeem its bonds on June 1, 1990. In at par in 1970, out at par in 1990, if you stayed the course, clipped your coupons, and just enjoyed the 6 percent tax free. Through thick and thin.

Just to make a point about getting-in and getting-out costs, if you bought the 6s of '90 when they were issued on June 1, 1970, and wanted to sell the very next day, you would have received a bid from us of $980 per thousand, the normal two-point spread between "bid" and "ask" in those days.

Selling two years later, when President Nixon had imposed wage and price controls and hopes of staunching inflation were high, the resale price would have been $1,110 per thousand. You'd have made $110—plus the 6 percent interest you had been collecting.

In the New York City fiscal crisis four years later, the bid had fallen to 82, $820 per thousand. But if you held on until the 1978–79 recession, you'd have gotten all your money back. 100! But, only for a short time. In the brunt and aftermath of the great inflation with new bonds coming to market at 10 percent ... 11 percent ... 12 percent ... 13 percent, and more—tax free!—the NYS 6s with fewer than ten years to run, were bid at their all-time low of 64, a loss of $360 per thousand.

The rest is history. If you had held through thick and thin to June 1, 1990, the date of maturity, you'd cash in at full face value, 100, winding up with the promised 6 percent, tax free, yield to maturity—from all the interest for twenty years ($1,200), plus your original $1,000 back.

So, there's one answer to, how much will I lose? The price you pay for a fixed-income security the day you buy it locks in your yield to maturity for however many years that bond has to run. No matter how much interest rates fluctuate, the interest your bond pays you stays the same. Your yield to maturity is fixed unless you sell. In that case, your bonds must compete with interest rates on new issues coming along. To sell your bond, its resale price in the open market adjusts—up or down—in line with new bonds coming into the muni market.

Anyone investing in municipal bonds faces this question: Is this a good time to be buying munis? Take with a grain of salt any investment advice based on pronouncements of where interest rates will be tomorrow. No one can tell you with a straight face where interest rates are going. The one measurement we do have of the relative attractiveness of municipal bonds is a number called the "tax-free-to-taxable-yield ratio"—comparing munis to taxable alternatives of comparable quality and maturity.

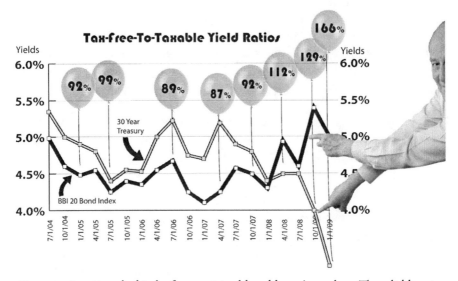

You are witnessing the birth of a municipal bond buyer's market. The solid line is an average of the yields to maturity of twenty representative long-term municipal bonds. The shaded line represents thirty-year Treasury yields. Where the two lines cross in early 2008 and wind up in 2009, munis top Treasuries without even taking the value of tax exemption into account. Historically, tax-free municipal bonds yield 80 percent to 90 percent of Treasuries. Above a tax-free-to-taxable yield ratio of 100 percent, munis are a screaming buy compared to Treasuries.

At this moment of writing, January 8, 2009, the formal tally of the Electoral College has been counted, certified by Congress, and Obama is declared elected President of the United States with 365 out of 538 votes. As of January 8, 2009, the deficit for the current fiscal year is $1.2 trillion, not including any money that will be spent on a rescue plan for the economy, which Obama has already proposed at $775 billion. Credit is nonexistent. Despite daily chaos, the Dow is virtually unchanged at 8,742. High-grade, AA-rated thirty-year municipal bonds are yielding 5.02 percent—tax free—as opposed to 3.03 percent for the thirty-year Treasuries—federally taxable. The tax-free-to-taxable-yield ratio has been turned on its head. Municipal bonds, which normally yield 80 percent to 90 percent of Treasuries, are yielding 166 percent of Treasuries, making them a screaming buy with respect to the past and to Treasuries as your taxable alternative.

One hitch with the tax-free-to-taxable-yield ratio. A snapshot at a moment in time comparing one fixed-income security to another fixed-income security ducks the real question, where are interest rates for both of them headed? Locking in a rate of return for the next ten years (no matter how safe) can be a scary commitment.

So, one of the money games people love to play is waiting for interest rates to go up. The wish being father of the thought, lenders always think interest rates are going up. And they're right. Of course, interest rates are going up, then down, then up, up down, down up. Speculating on interest rates is irresistible, because, at some point, you'll be right— if you play the waiting game long enough. The worst thing that could happen is to be right the first time and be fooled by intimations of infallibility. The advice of this expert: take any investment advice based on foretelling the future of interest rates, including mine, with a grain of salt. If I tell you, "Wait, or stay short, I think interest rates are going up," stuff wax in your ears and tie yourself to the mast. I may be right, but I have no way of knowing.

Here's a dependable prediction. If you invest regularly, you will hit some markets, you will miss some. Time may be a lousy beautician, but it's a great healer and the best friend an investor's got.

Time smoothes out the lumps.

Time gives the pendulum a chance to swing both ways.

Time gives a run of tails a chance to come up heads.

It changes the ups and downs of markets, which feel like forever, into just another day on the way to San Jose.

Time is the soul mate of investing. But trying to grab time by the big toe and nail the market is a fool's game. If you invest when you have the funds, you'll have your hands full enough just timing the toughest decision there is in municipal bonds: maturity. When do you want your money back?

Long bonds usually pay more.

Short bonds fluctuate less.

And therein is the dilemma—long vs. short—and good red meat for the next chapter.

4

Never All Short, Never All Long, Never All Wrong

2004. This is a "yield curve," a snapshot of where interest rates stood for AA-rated munis in December 2004—and the advantage at the time for extending maturity from one year going out to thirty.

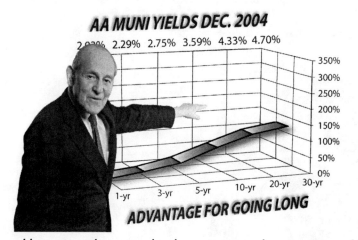

AA MUNI YIELDS DEC. 2004

2.03% 2.29% 2.75% 3.59% 4.33% 4.70%

350%
300%
250%
200%
150%
100%
50%
0%

1-yr   3-yr   5-yr   10-yr   20-yr   30-yr

ADVANTAGE FOR GOING LONG

You would expect a thirty-year bond to pay more than a one-year bond to compensate for the longer use the other fellow has of your money—and for additional uncertainty of what the future holds. The "yield curve" is the resulting snapshot at any moment in time of the reward for extending maturity, the reward expressed as a multiple of the one-year bond. Actual yields for each longer maturity appear at the top of graph.

From May 2000 to December 2004, the Federal Reserve has cut its short-term interest rate 13 times. The slope of the curve reflects the weight of all that easing, pushing interest rates down at the short end, while investor fears of inflation keep them up at the long end. By always starting each of these yield curves with the yield of the one-year bond on the base line, regardless of rate, and then plotting the yield of each longer bond as its percentage increase over the one-year, it is easy to compare changes in the steepening and flattening of the yield curve from one date to another. In December 2004, with the one-year muni paying 2.03 percent and the thirty-year at 4.70 percent paying 131% more than the one-year ... and two years later a mere 14% more ... you get the picture of long and short interest rates blowing in the winds of the changing economy.

2006. Two years later, the yield curve is flat as a pancake. The Federal Reserve has reversed monetary policy and ratcheted up short-term interest rates to cool off an overheated economy. But long-term rates haven't budged. In fact they have declined. Greenspan calls it a "conundrum."

With one-year Aa-rated munis at 3.49% and the thirty-year at 3.97 percent, the yield advantage for extending maturity is almost nil. The world is awash in liquidity and setting itself up for the subprime mortgage disaster.

2009. At the moment of writing in February 2009 with deficits in the trillions, the financial system a shambles, credit virtually nonexistent, the Federal Reserve has turned away from fighting inflation to fighting deflation and reliquifying the credit markets.

AA MUNI YIELDS FEB 2009

.62% 1.43% 1.91% 2.99% 4.54% 4.83%

350%
300%
250%
200%
150%
100%
50%
0%

1-yr 3-yr 5-yr 10-yr 20-yr 30-yr

ADVANTAGE FOR GOING LONG

The Fed Funds rate is practically zero. In lockstep, one-year AA-rated munis are paying 0.62 percent. Market forces have pushed thirty-year yields to 4.83%. With 7.79 times the return for extending maturity, the long end of the yield curve is literally "off the charts."

There is no telling what the yield curve will look like by the time this book is in your hands. But for now, the nine-year cycle of easing, tightening, easing since May 2000 is complete, leaving you with the same two dilemmas that were in your lap nine years ago. Dilemma one: Buy now or lay low? Dilemma two: Stay short or buy long?

As for buying now or buying later, the yield curve has all the predictive value of the Oracle at Delphi deciphering bird entrails. Too many forces, large and small, tug and pull on interest rates in different directions at the same time. Just when you think you've got it right, along comes one of those unpredictable shocks that Nassim Taleb writes about in *The Black Swan: The Impact of the Highly Improbable.* Could you have foreseen 9/11, or lesser cataclysms that have left their mark on markets and mankind: the wipeout of Bear Stearns and Lehman, collapse of A.I.G., Fannie, Freddie, and Merrill Lynch?

Until we get a better divination from Delphi, the best advice on investment timing comes from Sayra, Lebenthal's Founding Mom: "The time to invest is when you have the funds. You'll hit some markets. You'll miss some. Over the long haul, you'll average out." Mother didn't even know the words "dollar cost averaging." She practiced dollar cost averaging with her own money, because it made just "plain good horse sense, dear," and came to her naturally.

Same thing goes for dilemma two: maturity. Is March 2009's yield advantage for going long and locking in 7.79 times the return for staying short a buying opportunity or a come-on? Or is it even relevant to the all-important question? When will you have to put your hands on this money again? Long vs. short is a matter of matching maturity to your needs.

For all the ruckus in the yield curve, if it's money you know you're going to need in two, five, ten years, buy bonds that mature in two, five, ten years. If it's money you haven't touched in years and aren't likely to touch—"ladder" maturities with bonds coming due right along. If rates have come down, as bonds in your portfolio commence maturing, you will still have the longer bonds in your portfolio working at the higher rates. If rates have gone up, you'll be reinvesting at even higher rates, keeping your portfolio abreast of the market. If it's any consolation to you, no matter what happens with interest rates, you have a chance of never being more than half wrong.

"It makes plain good horse sense, dear. Never all short, never all long, never all wrong."

The Weight of Inflation on Real Rates of Return

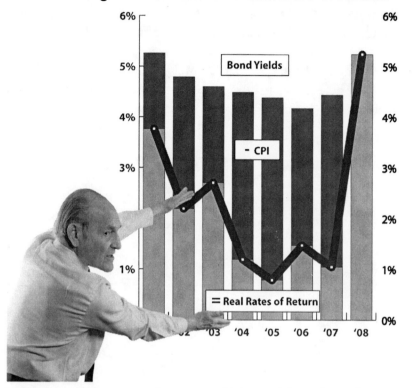

It's not how much you earn that counts. It's how much you keep after taxes and inflation. Tax-free municipal bonds eliminate taxes from the equation. But inflation comes right off the top. Using Bond Buyer 20-Bond Index (black + shaded) to represent long-term munis and the Consumer Price Index (CPI) to represent inflation (black), the real rate of returns after inflation (BBI – CPI = RRR) ranged from 3.76 percent in 2001 … to a low of 0.78 percent in 2005 … to a high of 5.24 percent in 2008, when the CPI was 0 percent and the full yield of the bond all take-home pay. Or, so it was for at least for 2008.

In coping with inflation, our cities and states don't have the same luxury of printing money to cover the open-ended liability available to the Treasury with its TIPS (Treasury Inflation Protected Securities). TIPS keep abreast of inflation by adjusting return of principal at maturity for changes in the CPI. Instead, the muni market constantly feels its way along, adjusting the offering price of new issues and the resale value of outstanding bonds for inflation anticipated in the future.

Not a very precise science. In that imprecision, whether you win or lose depends on the severity and length of the inflation cycle. You win, if, as, and when inflation abates, and you go right on clipping a high coupon rate that you locked in when it looked like inflation would be forever. You lose, if the cycle persists and you have to sell your bonds at a discount before they mature. A compelling excuse for diversifying maturities as well as municipalities: *never all short, never all long, never all wrong.*

5

Degrees of Sincerity in the Commitment to Pay

THE GO PLEDGE of full faith and credit, backed by the obligation to levy taxes for debt service on all real taxable property, unlimited as to rate or amount, is the ultimate in sincerity of commitment to pay. Sovereigns also have a pragmatic reason to make good. They have to preserve their credit. They are always building something else and selling you new bonds. They need their credit to provide for the continuation of life in the future. The claim the future has on the present explains why Chicago paid police officers and schoolteachers in scrip during the Depression, but bondholders in cash. It's why New York City, during the moratorium on its notes, broke its neck to salvage what was left of its credit and make good on its bonds. Credit. You can't govern without it.

So, it's both too bad and a good thing, too, that GOs constitute only 30 percent or so of the new issue market these days. Laws on the books that limit the amount of this unlimited, tax-backed stuff an issuer is allowed to have outstanding are one of the strengths going for the GO. In New York State, that ceiling is 10 percent of the average full value of real property over the most recent five years. Another strength: voters have to approve new GO issues. That's what those bond propositions on the ballot are all about. I can think of only one way to gild the GO lily: take debt service out of the hands of the issuer entirely, and secure it with U.S. Treasury bonds. So let me explain pre-refunding.

Pre-Res. When an issuer sets out to take advantage of low interest rates by refinancing a bond issue that is still not eligible for an optional call, the issuer floats a new bond issue and sequesters the proceeds in an unbreakable escrow account invested in U.S. Treasury bonds, for the sole purpose of paying off the old bond issue when it can be called. The old issue is now "pre-refunded." It also had been "defeased," meaning it no longer weighs on the back of the issuer for payment of debt service, but on the "absolute, unconditional, and irrevocable" promise of the escrow account to pay. With Uncle Sam's collateral behind the pre-re, you now own a tax-exempt municipal bond secured by the safest of the safe, those bonds of the U.S. government. Not to quibble, the ultimate obligor is still the escrow account. Uncle Sam pays the Treasuries. The escrow account owes you.

Revenue Bonds. When a bond is secured by project earnings, tolls, rentals, mortgage payments, admissions, ticket sales, fares, fees, tuitions—in other words, by charges to the user instead of by taxes—it is said to be a revenue bond. The strength of the revenue bond lies in the power of a government agency to price and charge for a necessity of life. That can be tantamount to the power of the GO issuer to tax, especially when the issuer is obliged to increase its tolls or charges so revenues exceed debt service by healthy margins of safety ... and there are strict limits on the issuance of additional bonds. All the same, revenue bonds must be judged on their commercial and economic viability, since citizens may pay to use the facility or not, as they see fit, in good times or bad.

In the decade of the 1990s, the reported default rate of hospital revenue bonds at $545.8 million amounted to just under 5/100ths of 1 percent of the average $1.13 trillion municipal bonds of all types outstanding. For multifamily housings, defaults at $2.05 billion, came to 18/100ths of 1 percent of outstanding munis. For water, gas, and sewer bonds, defaults at $39.4 million work out to less than 4/1000ths of 1 percent. For college and university revenue bonds, the default rate at $10.5 million was less than 1/1000 of 1 percent. (Triple-A Princeton University 4 1/2s of 2037 anybody?)

Asset-Backed Bonds. When the asset behind a municipal bond is a dependable source of revenue, such as the sales tax or personal income tax, a highway trust fund, or state aid, that bond can be as good for the money as a GO—and even more secure when the asset is not permitted to be used for any other purpose until the bonds have been paid. Some asset-backed bonds are rated as high or higher than a state's own GOs, despite one less angel they have dancing on the head of the pin: unlike general obligation bonds for which debt service *must* be appropriated, debt service on asset-backed bonds is subject to annual appropriation by the legislature. Notwithstanding the appropriation requirement, the default rate of asset-backed bonds has been zero.

Appropriation Bonds. In different states, an agency of the state issues bonds to finance construction of a public facility for use by the state. The agency then leases the facility back to the state and uses the rental it receives to pay debt service on the construction bonds. The lease securing the bonds may be "absolute and unconditional," but, because one legislature may not bind the next to appropriate revenues in a future session, and one year's appropriation has no force on the next, the rent is subject to *re*-appropriation every year. Would the legislature ever not appropriate? Would it not pay the rent on the prison, the state university, the state capitol? Let the philosophers debate would they, could they? Appropriation bonds are usually rated one notch below the GOs of the state itself. All the same, the default rate for appropriation bonds has also been zero.

Journalists rail at the lack of transparency in the municipal bond market. How are tax collections going? How much of the annual budget goes for debt service? Does the town borrow for operating expenses? Are bondholders protected against dilution of debt service coverage? The information is obtainable. You can google anything in this day and age. And you can get answers from the horse's mouth in the tell-all pages of the Official Statement—the issuer's disclosure document for new issues available by e-mail from the issuer or from your broker for the asking.

What's lacking is the profit motive and incentive for investors to do the same kind of research on their bonds investors willingly do in the hopes of doubling their money in the stock market. If it's naïve to think you're going to look under the hood and go digging in an Official Statement, at least you can kick the tires and still get a pretty good feel for a bond from its rating, type, essentiality, and from a suitability test of a different kind, its explicability to one's spouse.

Ratings. At the rating agencies, numbers go in, letters come out that grade an issuer's financial operations, local economy, demographics, debt load, availability of revenues for paying debt service, and legal safeguards protecting the bondholder, in short, its "creditworthiness." The upper four ratings (for example S&P's AAA, AA, A, BBB) are considered, in varying degree, "investment grade." In spite of a few spectacular defaults—$2.25 billion Washington Public Power Supply System revenue bonds in 1983, $800 million Orange County, California, GOs in 1994—the safety that attracts one to municipal bonds in the first place is present in all four ratings. But the disparity of yields among ratings seems to wave a red flag. "Uh oh! Only A, or worse, BBB? Sounds like something must be wrong."

A constant criticism is that munis, which rarely default, are held to a higher standard by the rating agencies than corporate bonds, which, as a category, are shakier. A muni with the same unlikelihood of defaulting as a corporate bond might be rated A, while the corporate gets away with a AA. The double standard socks the states and municipalities with higher and unfair costs of borrowing. California is suing, and a bill has been in Congress that would require the rating agencies to rate municipal bonds and other securities solely on likelihood of repayment. Even though more AAs and AAAs could pop up in any new rating system, let me tell you what I look for when I get up and go public on Lebenthal.com with our "Bond of the Day."

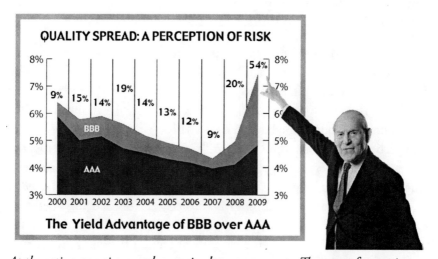

At the rating agencies, numbers go in, letters come out. The upper four ratings— AAA, AA, A, BBB (Fitch and Standard & Poor's) and Aaa, Aa, A, Baa (Moody's)—are all "investment grade," ranging from very, very, very good to good. (For rating definitions, see Glossary.) Ratings reflect evaluation of risk. On the other hand, the changing differences in yield—from BBBs paying 9 percent more than AAAs in 2000 to 54 percent more in 2009—reflect mood swings of the market. In 2009, investors switched from chancing the higher yield of lesser-rated bonds to running for the hills and the peace of mind of AAAs.

Ultimate Obligor. When all is said and done, who owes you the money? The state? Or, in the case of those lease rental appropriation bonds, the agency of the state? Have you ever been confused by a seeming contradiction like this in a disclosure statement? The state's rental payments securing the bonds are "absolute and unconditional," and then, when the document goes on to emphasize that the bonds are not (repeat not) a debt of the state, have you ever thought, *Whoa! That's double-talk?* It's not double-talk, if you connect the dots. The state's debt obligation is not to the bonds or to you the bondholder. It's obligation for those rental payments securing the bonds is to the agency. Although the revenue for bond payment may come from the state, the agency is your ultimate obligor. It's a fine point for the benefit of the broker to know, in order to avoid the pitfall of pitching an appropriation bond as a debt owed to you by the state. The agency owes you. That's why appropriation bonds, being that step removed from a state obligation to the bondholder, are usually rated one notch below the state's own GOs that indeed are debt of the state.

Essentiality. I look for a public purpose so imbued with essentiality, the issuer must do whatever it takes to preserve its credit. That's why I'm big on Metropolitan Transportation Authority (MTA) bonds for the New York City subways. Regardless of their A2/A rating, MTA Transportation bonds are backed every which-what way: by a prior lien on fare box collections, then Triboro Bridge and Tunnel tolls, dedicated operating revenues, mortgage recording taxes, state and city aid, etc. But I do worry when the GO pledge of prior lien, full faith, credit, and the municipality's unlimited taxing power are used for operating expenses, expendables, and deficit financing. Perverting the GO for deficit financing is stealing the blessing intended for good bonds that build infrastructure and bestowing it on the daily costs of running the town, with nothing to show for the money once it's spent.

Type of bondholder protection. GO, revenue, asset-backed, appropriation ... I want to know where the bondholder stands in line when it comes to getting paid. From having a prior lien on all the issuer's revenues ... to having a secondary lien after operating expenses and maintenance have been paid ... to an *executory* lien. Unlike the GO, executory means bondholders get paid from available revenues. If the cupboard is bare and the wherewithal just plain isn't available, the issuer doesn't have the same legal obligation to do what the Court insisted New York City do in overturning the moratorium: go out and generate the revenues to pay!

Explicability to one's spouse. I'm from the Warren Buffett (also Sayra Lebenthal) School of Good Horse Sense. If you can't explain a tender option bond (TOB) to your spouse, it's the Lord's way of saying leveraged derivatives aren't for you. Let me try you out with Municipal Bondom's equivalent of Fermat's Last Theorem:

A city issues $100,000,000 thirty-year bonds and buys municipal bond insurance guaranteeing payment. The bonds become triple-A, an absolute necessity to open up the market for a very special investor: the money market funds. But first we need a trust to buy up all $100,000,000 and turn $95,000,000 of them into "floaters."

They're called floaters because the trust adjusts the interest rate of the $95,000,000 up or down weekly. That maintains market value steadily at par so the floaters won't "break the buck" in the portfolio of the money fund client. And for ready liquidity, the floaters come with a "put," so the money funds can tender them back to a remarketing agent at any readjustment date at par to meet redemptions. Now, here's where the leverage comes in.

The other $5,000,000 worth of the bonds go to a hedge fund or investor who might never before have given dull, stodgy municipal bonds a thought in passing but is wooed by the prospect of leveraging return on investment, eight ... nine ... ten times. How so? Because the investor in the $5,000,000 remnant, called "inverse floaters," will get the inverse—what's left of all the fluctuating tax-free interest being paid each week to the money fund that bought the $95,000,000 floaters minus expenses paid to the liquidity provider, remarketing agent, and trustee fees.

The investor in the $5,000,000 inverse floaters has the effective benefit of owning the whole $100,000,000 block of bonds on a hugely leveraged basis, being entitled, to the remaining interest on the $95,000,000 after the various deductions. To hedge volatility on the whole $100,000,000, the investor in the inverse floater enters into an interest rate swap.

So what could go wrong? The triple-A bond insurance rating could be downgraded due to mortgage exposure, making them no longer money market eligible. Short-term rates on the $95,000,000 floaters could go up, leaving less than nothing for owner of the remnant inverse floater. The market could fall out of bed on the whole $100,000,000 of the long maturities. And the cost of the hedge could go up. Everything could go wrong. And it did. TOBs today are worth a fraction of original investment—if you can even get a bid at all.

Now, if you can explain the inexplicable to your spouse at dinner tonight, have I got a deal for you! Dirt cheap. But if you can't, lucky you. It means somebody up there likes you and is telling you to cut a wide swath around the inexplicable. Let's just say that TOBs, or for

that matter, anything else you don't get and can't explain, are just not
for you.

6

How Much is That in Dollars?

DON'T BE UPSET if all the talk in billions-trillions makes you feel like a bump on a log. You're not alone. In fact, no activity can have as much impact on the nation's $14 trillion economy as savers, just like you, investing and turning their dollars into new tools of production that create real wealth and pay off in benefits for generations to come.

Want to feel better? Sit in on a conference call of an underwriting syndicate working up the coupon rates and reoffering prices of a new bond issue. It's a billion dollar deal. The syndicate is working for a profit of four basis points—4/100ths of 1 percent of $1,000,000,000. Even masters of the universe are stumped when one of them asks, "In dollars, how much are we working for?" So the geniuses start asking each other, "Four million?" "Four hundred thousand?" "Forty something … I know it's got a four in it." And so it goes.

If that sounds like you, classroom come to order. Even if math isn't your best subject, let's turn a municipal bond into cold, hard cash. On the radio, our Bond of the Day would sound like this:

> We own and offer, subject to prior sale and/or change in price, $100,000 triple-A-rated New York State Environmental Facilities Corporation Water Pollution Control State Revolving Fund Revenue

5 percent bonds of 2022 at a 4.35 percent yield to a par call in 2017 and 4.54 percent yield to maturity. Price approximately 104 5/8.

Forget, for the moment, that the Environmental Facilities Corporation Bonds—EFCs—are rated triple-A by all three recognized rating agencies (on their own merits without municipal bond insurance).

Forget that the EFCs are for a noble, green, public purpose— cleaning up our rivers and streams.

Forget that they are secured by multiple layers of bondholder protection, on top of which a third or half the money to pay them off at maturity is already on hand.

Just focus on the money: par, coupon rate, yield to maturity, yield to call, approximate price expressed in dollars and cents.

In a print advertisement, the EFCs would look like this:

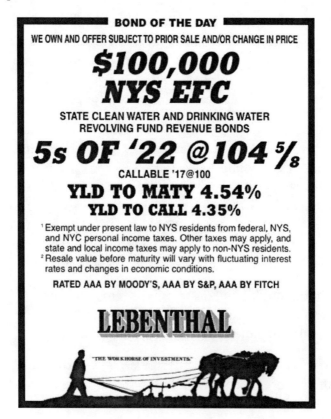

$100,000

PAR VALUE: $100,000 is face value of that portion of the original $218,830,000 issue that came to market in 2007 and is now reoffered by us to you in the secondary market.

5s

COUPON RATE: At 5 percent, each $1,000 of face value pays $50 a year, or $25 every June 15 and December 15, until maturity or call date. That amounts to $5,000 a year on the whole $100,000, free of federal, NYS, and NYC income tax.

'22

MATURITY DATE: June 15, 2022, is when the last interest payment will be made, and the bonds would be redeemed for $100,000. (Unless they were called for redemption prior to maturity at full face value at the option of the Environmental Facilities Corporation, allowed by the terms of the original deal.)

104 5/8

APPROXIMATE DOLLAR PRICE: The $100,000 block of bonds, quoted roughly as 104 5/8, are actually being quoted as an approximate percentage of face value, or, to be precise, 104.625 percent of $100,000, which works out to $104,625. Who would pay $104,625—a premium of $4,625—for $100,000 worth of 5 percent bonds, knowing they are going to get back only the $100,000 at the end? A connoisseur of municipal bonds looking for a 5 percent coupon to live on. That's who. The premium you pay is not a loss, because in fact, you *do* get it back, bit by bit, every six months in your interest payment. Between getting your interest right along and par at the end, you wind up with the yield to call or the yield to maturity you were quoted. No loss!

Callable '17 @ 100 and Yld to Call 4.35 Percent

CALL DATE AND PRICE AND YIELD TO CALL: Commencing June 15, 2017, the New York State Environmental Facilities Corporation may, at its option, redeem the bonds at par (100) and bump you out of the picture. If they did, you would be getting back face value five years ahead of time. That would mean five fewer years of enjoying the 5 percent coupon. Instead of the 4.54 percent yield to maturity in 2022, you would have earned a 4.35 percent yield to the call in 2017.

Yld to Maty 4.54 Percent

YIELD TO MATURITY: If the Environmental Facilities Corporation doesn't exercise its option to call the bonds, and they run all the way to maturity in 2022, between the cash flow from your 5 percent interest every six months and cashing in the bond itself at par (100), you will earn a yield to maturity of 4.54 percent.

4.78%

CURRENT YIELD (NOT SHOWN): Sometimes known as the dividend yield of a bond. If all you care about is how much you will be earning on your investment every time you clip a coupon, just divide the 5 percent coupon rate by the 104 5/8 cost. The current yield of the EFCs works out to 4.78 percent, which is nice to know if you are living on income. It's not shown, because part of that current yield is your own money, the return of premium you paid up front. And one other thing not shown:

Accrued Interest

If you buy a bond on anything other than an interest payment date, your confirmation will show an adjustment for the interest accrued before you entered the picture on the next coupon, which the previous owner is entitled to. Since the bond will be in your possession when the coupon comes due, you reimburse the previous owner beforehand. (Just as someone buying a bond from you would have to reimburse you for interest already accrued while the bond was in your hands.)

Incidentally, the underwriting team in our opening homily was working for $400,000.

7

When the Flag Touches the Ground

MUNICIPAL BOND DEFAULTS are few and far between. But when a rare one does go belly up (or runs afoul of one rotten egg's venality), all municipal bonds get yanked out of obscurity and dragged in the mud. The public may not be able to tell you exactly where the money for their school or bridge, sewer or subway, came from. But when New York City declares a moratorium on paying off $1.6 billion notes or a crooked firm brings a score of phony deals to market totaling more than a billion dollars with no intention of doing anything with bond proceeds except to pocket the money being earned in the "construction fund," it makes front page news. Suddenly the taxpayers wake up, and an outraged citizenry comes to life.

As a bond buyer, what skin is it off your nose that a bond you don't even own of some faraway place with a strange-sounding name plummets in price? Plenty! In public finance, the loss of trust by the public in how its money is being handled takes every bond down a peg. Even if the hit to municipal bond prices across the board is only one basis point—1/100 of 1 percent on the $2,700,000,000,000 bonds outstanding—that is still a stiff $270,000,000 in market value tossed out the window.

Municipal bonds are particularly vulnerable to market risk. One New York City fiscal crisis, "Whoops" affair, Orange County, or bond cheat can have an impact across the board. Rather than a stirrer-upper with no solutions, let me be the one to expose the skeletons in our closet.

Case of Munching on Seed Corn

The next time you come in for a landing at LGA, ORD, or LAX at night, look down at those pinpoints of light passing under the wing. And conjure up that mealy mouthed word infrastructure—the highways and bridges, transportation systems, and public works that provide the physical underpinnings for our quality of life.

Photography by Paul Chesley

Spaghetti bowl Chicago at night

Infrastructure is capital that creates more capital. It's seed corn. You plant it. It grows. Or, as the economist Robert Heilbroner put it in *21ˢᵗ Century Capitalism,* "Capital is wealth whose value does not inhere it its physical characteristics, but in its use to create a larger amount of wealth. Typically this takes place as money is converted into commodities such as raw materials, the raw materials converted into finished goods and services, and the finished goods sold on the market—to buy more raw materials and start the process all over again."

Demeaning municipal bonds, using them to borrow for papers and pencils, salaries and pensions, with nothing to show for the money once it's spent, pulls the plug on that process of capital replenishment. It's like Farmer Brown sitting down at the dinner table, tucking in his bib, and eating the seed corn. Tired of the old seed-corn metaphor? Then call using municipal bonds for deficit financing just quenching someone's thirst with saltwater. You know they're going to pay for that drink of saltwater later—and then some. Just the way New York City had to pay in the seventies, when Hugh Carey and Abraham Beame, the governor of New York State and the mayor of New York City, respectively, had to troop off to Washington, hats in hand, pockets inside out, to beg the federal government for a loan.

FORD TO CITY – DROP DEAD, the famous <u>New York Daily News</u> headline, at first said it all. Nevertheless, the City got its $2.5 billion federal loan guarantee -- at a humiliating price. Demonic as it sounds, the City would have to rub its own nose in the mess of its profligate ways, by declaring the moratorium and in front of the world suffering the ignominy of defaulting on $1.6 billion worth of New York City general obligation notes. After a year, the Court ruled the default unconstitutional. That year gave the city breathing room to pay off the notes, repay Treasury and begin a decade of getting its house in order. But it was a decade of layoffs, overcrowded classrooms, shuttered fire stations, garbage piling up, subways breaking down, crime going up. Even being forced to get rid of that grating give-away to the city's immigrants and poor, *free* tuition at City College, since 1847 an incubator for hatching greats from the teeming masses.

The Old Brother-in-Law Test. Dressing up borrowing to paper over deficits with general obligation bonds dilutes a municipality's ability to pay debt service on *all* of its bonds, the good ones for productive investment and the bad ones for everyday expenses. The debtor's yields get juicier and juicier. It's a warning something's wrong. Give those bargain bonds the same test you would if your brother-in-law put the arm on you for a loan. Ask what the money is for. If it's for plugging holes in the budget—no new subway, no new school, no new water mains—why should you be the one to dilute the issuer's credit even more? Always remember, Uncle Sam may have a printing press and can inflate his way out of a hole. But our municipalities have to pay off their debts out of the productivity gains that come from the return on investment in *infrastructure*.

Whoops!

What would you call the biggest municipal bond default in U.S. history? You'd call it a lot worse than "whoops!" if you were left holding the bag for $2.25 billion in Washington Public Power Supply System—WPPSS—bonds, which in the process of invalidating, the Court, putting it mildly, called "a mistake," a "frustration of purpose," and an "impracticality."

In the Pacific Northwest of the 1970s, the federal Bonneville Power Administration was warning, no more cheap, abundant energy in the region—unless the public utilities got together and participated in building two huge new nuclear energy plants, the now infamous WPPSS Project 4 and 5 plants.

If Projects 4 and 5 bonds had been revenue bonds, pure and simple, paid solely from sales of power, default would come under the heading "inability to pay." With no sales, there would be no revenues. But WPPSS 4 and 5 bonds were backed by a security mechanism called "take-or-pay." Eighty-eight municipal- and investor-owned utilities in Washington, Oregon, and Idaho jointly promised to pay construction costs, including debt service, whether or not the plants got built and produced energy. Where would the utilities get the money? From their regular customers, eating the costs, buried in their higher and higher bills for electricity.

"These were the go-go years," wrote our trade paper, *The Bond Buyer*'s Howard Gleckman. "No one wanted to lose a potential new factory because it could not guarantee enough electricity to keep the plant operating. By signing the take-or-pay agreement, each utility would receive its share of the abundant new power." And their regular electricity customers, not investors, would be the ones taking on the risk of a "dry hole."

All the while that higher and higher electric bills were arriving in the mail, the promise of cheap, clean nuclear energy was fading fast. With the Three Mile Island nuclear accident in Pennsylvania, the fall of nuclear power from grace, a flip-flop from oil scarcity to oil surplus, and construction cost overruns so great that none of the plants could ever produce electricity economically, the good people of the Pacific Northwest got up on their hind legs and howled at those electric bills. WPPSS amounted to giving bondholders a blank check and saddling rate payers with unlimited debt they'd never voted for. The courts agreed that without a popular vote, the bonds were illegal. On June 15, 1983, the Washington Supreme Court declared WPPSS bonds, not just a "mistake," "frustration of purpose," and an "impracticality," but also *invalid*.

This wasn't just New York City or an Asbury Park, New Jersey, going broke and having to default. It was *repudiation* of debt, an out-and-out unwillingness to pay. By 1995—after twelve long years of waiting—bondholders picked up seven or eight cents on the dollar. They received another thirty cents from settlement agreements with security firms and bond attorneys who had deemed take-or-pay legal in the first place. Cold comfort to bondholders that take-or-pay had been ruled legal in other states. Public policy in the states of Washington, Oregon, and Idaho had settled the clash between the obligatory and the impossible, as though the debt had never existed. Public Policy— that elusive, ephemeral, ineffable notion of what was good and what was bad for the Pacific Northwest—became a pair of wild cards that trumped even sanctity of contract. My takeaway: the commitment of public credit for a public purpose is a powerful expression of something the public believes in. Not just the words on paper, but in the concrete thing being "built by bonds." If the people haven't voted for it and aren't for it, whoops!

"Abba Dabba Do" and the Little Black Box

What do you get when you cross the mind of a master deal maker with the heart of a horse thief? You get an "Abba Dabba Do," the nickname the trading desk wags gave investment banker Arthur Abba Goldberg, before he was hit with an eighteen month jail sentence.

In 1985 and 1986, Goldberg, as executive vice president of the long gone underwriting firm Matthews & Wright, Inc., fabricated $1,484,000,000 worth of sham municipal bonds for territorial Guam and such obscure entities as the Sac and Fox tribe of Indians of Oklahoma, the trust territory of the Pacific Island Republic of Palau, and impoverished East St. Louis. And boy! Could East St. Louis use the idea Goldberg was floating: to build a $223,000,000 container port that would turn the local economy around. Except the port, the largest inland port in the whole wide world, was pure fantasy, never intended to see the light of day.

Without anyone (especially himself) putting up hard cash, Goldberg would "sell" his issuers' bonds to an unlicensed bank in Saipan, a mail drop in the Mariana Islands with no assets. In the shell bank, he would "deposit" checks that he had written on nonexistent funds in a credit union he had founded and controlled in the States. Without even depositing the checks, the bank would immediately endorse them back over to Goldberg to pay for the bonds. With nothing ever intended to be built, no real money changing hands or sticking to fingers, then why the charade? To beat the effective date of the arbitrage rebate provision imminent in the upcoming 1986 Tax Reform Act—and keep the door open for a way of minting money out of thin air.

Under this act, after August 31, 1986, municipal issuers would be required to rebate to Uncle Sam the profit from bond proceeds earning more while being invested in temporary construction accounts than the issuer's cost to borrow on the bonds. To avoid the arbitrage rebate, Goldberg and Matthews & Wright rushed anything to market that walked, talked, or crawled and warehoused the bonds in the proverbial black box in Saipan. Since the deals had closed before the deadline, they would be "grandfathered" and sold under the old rules, permitting arbitrage for up to three years. After August 31, 1986, Goldberg and Matthews & Wright would then remarket the bonds for *real* money and invest the proceeds of the remarketed bonds in higher-yielding guaranteed investment contracts (GICs). In three years, when the nonexistent project obviously failed to materialize, the deal would be collapsed, the remarketed bonds would be called in for redemption, and the escrow account would be closed. From a score of such collapsible bond deals, Goldberg and Matthews & Wright managed to walk away with $8,000,000 in underwriting fees from East St. Louis alone.

Odd what lets a cat get out of the bag. A federal indictment for bribery led to the SEC's nailing Goldberg and Matthews & Wright for securities fraud: failing to disclose their shenanigans in an offering of Matthews & Wright shares to the public. Matthews & Wright was fined $1,000,000 for the container port fraud, ordered to pay East St. Louis $7,000,000 in restitution for raising and dashing the city's hopes, and had its broker-dealer license revoked. Goldberg was banned from the securities industry for life, personally fined $100,000, and sentenced to eighteen months in prison. Total time served: six months. In the absence of bleeding bodies, white collar crime usually does tend to get off easy, and this is not a story about punishment fitting the crime. It's about future deterrence, for which Congress has handed the IRS an effective club. According to the *Bond Buyer*, the trade daily, "A day after the Guam bonds were issued, the IRS released revenue ruling 85-182 to put a halt to such collapsible escrowed bond issues. The ruling said that municipal bonds would not qualify for tax exemption if—at the time they were issued—there was no reasonable expectation that the project to be financed would ever be built." The IRS determined the Guam bonds (for military housing that never got built) were not tax exempt. Then, in negotiating a plea bargain with Guam, the IRS pulled its punch and let the tax-exempt status of the bonds stand and nailed Goldberg and Matthews & Wright without revoking the tax-free status of their remarketed bonds.

Rarely has the IRS had to go all the way in taxing an issue of municipal bonds after the fact. The threat alone has usually been enough to get cheaters to straighten up and fly right. Consider how the IRS stopped a racket called "yield burning" and got ninety-nine bond firms to play by the rules, just by the IRS twirling its billy club and smacking it against its palm.

Go Ahead, Make the Tax Collector's Day

As you know, when a municipality floats a new bond issue to pre-refund an older one, the proceeds are safely banked in an escrow account and earn interest until they're needed to pay off the older issue.

As we've just seen, under the arbitrage rebate provision of the 1986 Tax Reform Act, the amount of interest earned on those borrowed funds in excess of what it cost the municipality to borrow must be rebated to the IRS. Yield burning would be the seemingly victimless business of reducing the excess earnings in the escrow account down to nothing by deliberately overpaying—hence burning off the yield of the securities being purchased. No arbitrage earnings, no rebate. Right? And no skin off the issuer's nose. After August 31, 1986, the issuer couldn't have kept the arbitrage earnings anyway. Right?

The trouble with yield burning is that it's cheating the IRS by the amount overpaid to the escrow provider. And who knows what goes on under the table with all that ill-gotten gain floating around? In 1995, a suit brought by whistleblower Michael Lissak accused a number of Wall Street firms of engaging in yield-burning abuses in hundreds of advance refundings. In the year 2000, Lissak's suit resulted in sixteen Wall Street firms settling with the government. Eventually, eighty-three firms around the country voluntarily ponied up $500,000,000 of profits to the IRS. Well, not entirely voluntarily. What was behind the widespread urge of so many perps to come clean? The IRS twirled its club and whispered, "Read my lips." And they saw the shining light of Revenue Procedure Ruling 96-41.

Revenue Procedure Ruling 96-41 laid down the law. Issuers who did not disgorge yield-burning profits on their transactions within a year would be subject to investigation and audit and potentially the revocation of the tax-exempt status of the bonds involved. The threat worked. It made the cost of yield burning and lawsuits arising out of the loss of tax exemption, mandatory bond redemption, disgorgement of profits, prohibitive for any firm caught with dirty hands.

If you're worried about buying a tainted bond, try logging onto "EMMA," www.emma.msrb.org. "EMMA" is the Municipal Securities Rulemaking Board (MSRB) Electronic Municipal Market Access system's website. Issuers must file with EMMA, and make public for all to see, eleven different kinds of notices of material events. You can check up on any bond you've been offered by its CUSIP number (stands for Committee on Uniform Security Identification Procedure) and search, not just for an adverse tax ruling for yield burning (if the

IRS has caught wind of it), but for other deal breakers like an interest payment default that has already occurred, an unscheduled draw on debt service reserves, or the failure of a liquidity provider to perform. If those *why nots* were not disclosed to you before you said, "I buy," betcha the "house" will gracefully, albeit with a red face, let you out of the trade.

How One Man Could Bankrupt
the Richest County in California

Robert Citron was the preening, swaggering, self-obsessed treasurer of Orange County, California, from 1972 to 1994. For twenty-one of those golden years, he piled up a fabulous record managing the county's cash flow and the liquid assets of all of its 241 municipalities. He kept taxes low. He turned away municipalities outside the county begging him to take their money, too. At the height of his glory, he parlayed $7.5 billion of the county's cash management pool into a $20 billion portfolio. No one dared question his almighty judgment. (Except the guy running against him, of course.) Citron was a star until February 1994, when he defied the gods and made a bet against the Federal Reserve. And lost.

The strategy that got Citron to that $20 billion depended on interest rates staying low. He was investing in reverse purchase agreements, short-term derivatives, and then leveraging them to buy five-year U.S. Government Agency Notes. He had turned Orange County's liquid, short-term cash management pool into a long-term investment. In February 1994, the Fed began ratcheting up the short-term Fed Funds rate. That meant the cost of renewing the "repos" was going up, up, up, while at the same time, the value of the five-year collateral was plummeting.

Derivatives are only as good as the hand that wields them. And in a megalomaniacal contest of Citron's pride versus Fed monetary policy, Citron wielded his derivatives wildly, doubling and tripling his bets to cover losses his leverage was compounding. We know from the racetrack, "Scared money never wins!" The awful and the inevitable came. Margins were called. Collateral liquidated. And the $7.5

billion that had actually been invested in the pool was down by $1.69 billion to $5.8 billion. To staunch the bloodbath and save what was left of the pool, Orange County filed for bankruptcy and walked away from its debts. Eight hundred million dollars worth of double-A-rated Orange County general obligation school bonds, the blue chips of the bond business, went into default. Temporarily. A year and a half later, the county emerged from bankruptcy. Auto license fees and revenues that might have been earmarked for buses, parks, harbors, and roads now had to go to holders of twenty-year Orange County Recovery Bonds. Orange County paid the price of default in money, layoffs, and in public services forgone. By 2008, only $650 million of the $1.69 billion loss had been recovered.

Derivatives can hedge against losses. But leverage, with losses compounding upon losses, can go nuclear and wipe out everything. Selling derivatives to Citron with the public's money had all the benefits to society of plying a drunk with boilermakers. For its part in feeding the madness, Merrill Lynch settled with Orange County for $400 million, even though Merrill never admitted or denied guilt.

Because there was no indication of personal financial gain in it for Citron, just greed in the service of others, he got off with a $100,000 fine and the sentence of a year in jail, commuted to 1,000 hours of public service.

Hard Lesson Learned. Our local governments are not in business to get rich. They're in business to break even while providing essential public service and continuity. The twin objectives of cash management are safety of principal and liquidity: put a dollar in, get a dollar out. If that means giving up yield and performance, so be it. Leveraging and extending maturity to goose returns have no business in cash management, whether it's the municipality's money or your own.

These days, Orange County's Investment Policy Statement prohibits going out and borrowing just to turn around and reinvest the proceeds. It prohibits reverse repurchase agreements, which are interest rate bets, and forbids volatile structured notes and derivatives. The maximum allowable maturity of any portfolio instrument is thirteen months, and the average maturity of all portfolio instruments in the aggregate, on a dollar-weighted basis, must not exceed ninety days. Investments are marked to market on a daily basis. If the net asset value of either the County Pool or sister pool for schools is less than 99.5 cents on the dollar or greater than 100.5 cents on the dollar, portfolio holdings may be sold, as necessary, to maintain the ratio between 99.5 cents and 100.5 cents.

Try to Google the municipality you're considering, and see if you can bring up its cash management policy. If you're successful, you'll be able to compare it with that of Orange County, the sinner reformed. In 1998, Orange County won the Government Finance Officer's Award for financial reporting that covered all its operations. How's that for getting a fractious horse back in the barn? Well, almost. Because Orange County may never recover the $1 billion that the pool is still short from the Citron days. Or its former glory. Rich, fat Orange County, California, has earned itself the bond cynic's parry: if Orange County could go bust, then what *is* any good?

Nothing in life, and certainly in investing, is risk free. Anyone going into municipal bonds must accept some presence of risk. Market risk, credit risk, political risk, call risk, headline risk, taxability risk. Then again, as founder Sayra Lebenthal would say, "If you're going to worry about everything, dear, keep your money in a mattress—and don't smoke in bed."

The Blob
(Not The Movie But The Newsreel of California's Deficit)

"THE BLOB" IN the 1988 movie was "indescribable," "indestructible," "insatiable." Nothing could stop it. How can anything today stop the blob in the 2009 newsreel of the deficit that is eating California alive? I know one thing that could ... and that's cutting off the oxygen supply from the same sort of blob that was killing New York City in the seventies. How so? By depriving California of the credit it takes for deficit financing. As long as California knows it can borrow its way out of a hole, its budget impasse can drag on and on in the clash between those who oppose increasing taxes and those who oppose cutting services. California has already used up $15 billion of short term deficit financing, issuing Economic Recovery Bonds, authorized by the voters in 2004. And, at this very moment in June 2009, a plan is on the table for plugging another $24 billion shortfall in the state's 2010 fiscal year budget with billions more deficit bonds.

How long can California go on borrowing with no superhighway, no school, no water plant or sewer system to show for the money? Without credit, California would have no choice but to do involuntarily what it has been unable to do of its own free will. As Isaac B. Singer said when asked if he believed in free will, "Of course. I have no choice." Even if California cannot borrow its way out of the hole this time, and a *creditable*, balanced budget materializes out of thin air, California will still need another dose of what bit it, a short term loan to pay its bills. If you're thinking TARP, the U. S. Treasury has already said no to a bailout, although not with the tone of "Ford to City -- Drop Dead."

By the time *Lebenthal On Munis* is in your hands, we'll both know how the 2009 newsreel has turned out. One other thing that may help you decide, "Yes..." or "No!" about municipal bonds. The precepts in this book—about debt vs. deficit, the pragmatic necessity for sovereigns to preserve their credit, and the grip of infrastructure essentiality on commitment to pay—will have been put to an acid test, for the first time since the Great Depression.

8

Matching One You With A Million and a Half Possibilities

VOICES COME POURING out of the telephone:

"I have a child with special needs."

"I'm staying loose in case something else comes up."

"I'm going down in history as the best Nana ever."

"Let me hold it close to my chest and count it every night."

"I've got it timed so my last bond and I are redeemed on the same day."

"If I'm going to gamble, I'll go to Vegas."

"I did better than my parents, and I want my kids to do better than me."

"I didn't get here in a rocking chair, but I'm not the daredevil I was."

"I want to put it away, not touch it, come back one day, and what do you know, find it's still there and it earned a little something."

From what you say about *you*—your own wants, quirks, and idiosyncrasies—a good municipal bond man or woman will find out some things you didn't say. How likely are you to jump in and out of your bonds? Do you really need the income from your bonds now? How much is the peace and quiet of triple-A worth to you in cold cash? Is this money you're going to need in a pinch? Your answers will take a million and a half CUSIPs, representing every municipal bond in existence, and narrow them down to four basic investment decisions:

1. Should you go for triple-A or relax on rating and go for yield? The Rating vs. Yield Decision.

2. Do you want the full good of your investment here and now and every time you get your interest, or can you afford to defer return to maturity? The Income Now or Later Decision.

3. In your situation, which is better: the liquidity of short-term bonds or higher return of long-term bonds? The Long vs. Short Decision.

4. Should you pick and choose individual municipal bonds (and pay the "spread"), or buy a mutual fund of municipal bonds (and pay the annual fee)? The Do-It-Yourself vs. Management Decision.

Here's as much as I can put in writing without knowing more about you.

Decision One: Rating vs. Yield

Perception of the difference between an AAA-rating and just an A-rating makes the likelihood of default sound a lot worse than it is. But right now, when state and local governments are getting hit with declining tax revenues, isn't the time to be easing the rating system, as its critics propose. Just the same, a blind attachment to AAA means giving up more yield than you're gaining in quality. When choosing the Bond of the Day, I consider other things first: the essentiality of the infrastructure need served, its contribution to the local economy, where you stand in line to get paid— all those "Degrees of Sincerity in Commitment to Pay," described in chapter 6. Then I certainly pay attention to how Moody's and Standard & Poor's rate my choice. I am comfortable with the upper-four ratings (when I'm investing my own money) and the upper-three ratings when it's your money. (Look up "ratings" in the Glossary for Moody's rating definitions.)

Decision Two: Income Now vs. Income Later

When you're looking for current income to live on and want the most money from your investment every six months, then go for bonds with the highest coupon rate. Don't shy away from them just because you might have to pay a premium. That premium is part of your investment; it earns interest just as $1,001 in the bank earns interest on the $1 as well as the other $1,000. No, you don't get the premium back at the end, because you've been getting it back, bit by bit, every time you clip that big coupon.

But, if you don't need current income, consider the discount bond. (Just because a bond is selling at a discount doesn't mean it's in trouble.) The discount is what makes an issue with a low coupon rate competitive with a higher one. The market does this by pricing the discount bond at less than its face value. Part of the return on your investment will then come from the tax-free interest payments every six months and part from capital gains at maturity, subject to any tax due on gains.

The IRS considers the gain on a bond issued at an original issue discount (OID) as coming from the municipality and is therefore tax free. (Other long- or short-term gains above a certain amount, coming from the *market* to compensate for a change in interest rates or improvement in the fortunes of the issuer, are taxable as ordinary income.)

The quintessential OID would be a zero coupon bond. Take, for example, a $100,000 block of zero coupon bonds due in fifteen years selling at a discount of 4.75 percent to maturity. You would put in $49,471 now and get back the $100,000 at maturity—free of both income and capital gains taxes. Even though your current income from it is zero, your investment of $49,471 is effectively earning tax-free interest every six months at 4.75 percent per annum, building and rebuilding on itself at 4.75 percent. You must be the one to decide whether 4.75 percent tax free is a reinvestment rate you want to lock up—or be locked into—until maturity. In a roomful of experts, some will say interest rates are going up; others will say they're not. Who's right? Whomever you agree with, and that makes you one of the experts. After all, there is something about having your own money to invest that endows you with as much knowledge about where interest rates are going as anyone alive.

Decision Three: Long vs. Short (Tough One)

There is more to picking the right bond than just going for the highest yield. This is a business of give-ups. With short bonds, you can "cash in" in a couple of years instead of thirty; you are always close to your money. As they approach maturity, their market value is always approaching par, the face value they'll be worth at redemption. And there's your dilemma. Short bonds fluctuate less. But they pay less. Long bonds pay more. But they fluctuate more.

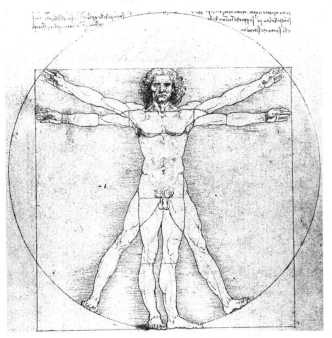

Da Vinci Vitruvian Man

Just think of fluctuation as Leonardo da Vinci's *Vitruvian Man*, swinging his outstretched arms up and down. Long bonds are at his fingertips, short bonds near his shoulder. With a change in interest rates a percentage point this way, a percentage point that, all points along his arms may travel in an arc the same number of degrees. But, the farther the bonds are from his shoulder, the greater the distance up and down along the arc those longer maturity bonds travel (analogous to price fluctuation). If you know when you need your money back, invest in bonds that mature accordingly. Don't subject your savings to an unnecessary swing in market price. If you have no real timetable for putting your hands on that money again, but just *might* need it unexpectedly, build a ladder of maturities that can return your investment at regular intervals. A fair warning: bond calls before maturity can alter the annual return of principal from maturing bonds that you had carefully planned on. So, for the purpose of laddering, I consider a twenty-year bond with a ten-year call a ten-year bond. I call a ten-year bond with a five-year call, a five-year bond … and so forth.

If you have no intention in your lifetime of spending the principal, you can get the most income by buying what I call "cash cows," long-term bonds with big, fat coupon rates. That way you'll get the superior current return in your lifetime. And when your bonds do come due, your principal will be returned to you or your heirs. You're going to leave an estate in some form. What difference whether you leave heirs money or municipal bonds that are worth money?

If you are getting on in years, do what I do. Build a "modified" barbell portfolio. Long-term bonds at one end of the portfolio have a higher yield when the yield curve is steep. And short bonds at the other end of the barbell provide market stability. Here's where the modified comes in. Instead of bunching all the short bonds in one year, ladder them over a comfortable span of one to five or six years. And go for the highest yields for the long end. All the way out to Kingdom Come, if it's money you have no intention of touching in your lifetime. After five or six years, all your original short bonds will be replaced at new rates of interest. Meanwhile, the long end of your barbell remains intact, earning the higher return you locked in when you began your portfolio. Once again, "Never all short. Never all long. Never all wrong."

Decision Four: Should You Build Your Own Portfolio or Hire a Manager to Build One for You?
("Hire" Is What You Do When You Buy a Municipal Bond Fund.)

There are two ways to build a municipal bond portfolio. One way is to pick up the phone, call a broker, get to know each other, and between the two of you, pick and choose individual bonds that make sense and feel right for you in your situation.

The other way is to buy a fund of bonds, let the fund manager balance ratings against yield, weigh coupons, maturities, and all that. You sit back and get your dividend interest, or—if you have the assets to make the economics work out—hire your own manager to tailor and manage a municipal bond portfolio for you.

Opting for management is a sign you could be seeking something more from the municipal bond market than just a nice, steady, tax-free income. (Although, what's wrong with that?) Let's face it. Bonds go up. And bonds go down. The investor in a managed account believes, "I'll do better warding against, or capitalizing on, the ups and downs of the bond market with a professional doing the buying, selling, holding, and trading rather than trying to anticipate interest rates on my own."

The retail investor scoffs, "Nobody can predict interest rates," and recites the mantra, "I don't buy to trade. I don't buy to trade." Having declared the intention to hold, the do-it-yourselfer then must face up to the toughest decision there is in municipal bonds: the long vs. short decision. The investor in an actively managed trading account has made his peace with maturity: a five-, ten-, twenty-year bond is actually no longer in maturity than the manager wants to hold onto it. If the manager decides to sell in one, two, or three years, he will ... at institutional spreads for as little as 50 cents to $2.50 or so per thousand (depending on maturity and the number of bonds).

For the do-it-yourselfer, retail spreads (the difference between what you pay us for a bond and what you would get if you sold it right back to us) can range from $2 to $15 per thousand (assuming there has been no change in interest rates). And that's another difference between building your own portfolio and hiring a municipal asset manager to build and manage one for you. To buy and hold, the retail investor pays the piper that spread between bid and ask just once. The *managed* investor pays a management fee every year, ranging from 0.25 percent to 0.50 percent (that is, 25 to 50 basis points) on assets under management in addition to a getting-in and getting-out cost of approximately 50 cents to $2.50 per thousand. If laddering maturities is the do-it-yourselfer's way of having money coming in regularly to keep abreast of interest rates, then buying, selling, trading in and out of long and short maturities is the manager's way of anticipating and coping with changing interest rates.

One final word about diversification. Your money is automatically diversified if you buy a mutual fund or choose personal municipal asset management. Whether you invest $500,000 or $5,000,000, your money gets spread over an assortment of issuers, localities, and market sectors. Spreading risk is not so easy for the under-$250,000 investor, who is picking and choosing bonds on his or her own. (Especially when the natural inclination is to do repeat business in a bond one has bought once and feels one knows.)

Avoid undue concentration. Diversification by itself doesn't ensure gains or protect against loss. But when you reach for yield, spread the risk, even if it means saying no to buying more of a bond you love. That's what the old Lebenthal always did best and what this book was written to do again: help investors decide, "Yes ... or No!"

9

The MuniProfiler

A Model of Lebenthal in a Bottle

DO YOU REMEMBER as a kid calling up the corner store and asking, "Have you got Prince Albert in a can ... well let him out?"

You invent the telephone, and what do you get? Prank calls.

You invent the MuniProfiler, and what do you get? People who want to play Matchups. People who could never bring themselves to pick up the telephone and bare their souls to a broker, wanting to simulate the head-to -head, heart-to-heart process of investing in municipal bonds -- by telling all to a computer.

You do that by logging onto www.lebenthal.com, filling out the questionnaire, and hitting submit. The MuniProfiler is a computer model that does what I do when I listen to someone's goals and analyze their tolerance for risk, need for cash flow, and need to put their hands on their money again. Only it does it faster and without my beady stare beating you into submission to buy. In nanoseconds the MuniProfiler searches for a combination of issuer, credit rating, coupon rate, and maturity. And up pops a model portfolio of municipal bonds, reflecting your needs, wants, and inclinations. If you want to change your answers, change them. Up pops a different bond portfolio, tailored to the new criteria.

You're welcome to log on free and experiment. One thing you will notice about the multiple choice questionnaire is that it does not push your bond expertise or make you go into the specifics of coupon, maturity, and rating to be looking for. The questions are looking for information about you.

"I want the best return I can get with the safety attracting me to municipals in the first place."

"A deal could come up. I could need my money at any time."

"I don't need income now. I prefer receiving my investment return in a big lump sum at the end."

The portfolio that comes up is then analyzed as a whole and averaged as to interest rate, maturity, annual cash flow, dollar price, and how much a taxable investment would have to pay to match it.

Happily, I won't ever have to sit at a keyboard again, hunting, pecking, fitting coupons, maturities, yields, and dollar prices neatly into columns. The MuniProfiler does it automatically for me. And zap! E-mails it to you. You, too, may like testing the waters, without getting your feet wet, until you're good and ready to talk to a broker..

10

Triple-A Insured
1971–2008

MUNICIPAL BOND INSURANCE was born in 1971. The first insured bonds were for a hospital in Greater Juneau, Alaska. From that time to 2008, the bond insurers, AMBAC, FGIC, FSA, and MBIA, had only one product for sale—confidence. I'm not talking about the confidence investors had in the insurers' ability to pay claims, but the confidence they got from the high tone of acclaim in the sound of "triple-A insured." For good reason, the insurance companies worshipped at the altar of the triple-A. It wasn't the reserves of $100 or so set aside—and eventually as little as $10—for every $1,000 of debt that inspired the confidence, but the third-party endorsement of Moody's, Standard & Poor's, and eventually Fitch IBCA.

The fire and casualty insurance companies understand catastrophe. They can project the number of cars that will have accidents, number of houses that will catch fire, number of crops that will be destroyed by hail—and build predictable losses into the premiums they charge for insurance. But municipal bond insurers underwrite to a zero loss standard. They have little incentive to go looking for trouble. That's because the rating agencies compel them to reserve capital for each insured issue in an amount depending on how risky it is. The riskier the issue, the more capital that has to be set aside and taken out of play. So, the insurers only guarantee municipal bonds that don't really need it. If a bond really did need insurance, other than to get that triple-A rating and bring down the cost of borrowing, believe me, the insurers would turn it thumbs down. And I ought to know. I was a director of MBIA, the premier municipal bond insurer.

After many profitable years of growth carrying coals to Newcastle by insuring bonds that don't need it, we began to get fidgety about our business. The saturation of triple-A bonds was affecting their market value. At some point, the cost of the insurance was going to wipe out the shrinking economic value of having it. We had to look elsewhere for future earnings and our growth.

Somewhere in Nantucket there's probably an antique store selling a bottle of genuine whale oil and an ancient lamp to go with it. Fine for the tourist industry, but Big Business cannot wallow in the past, *"withstand the logic of Wall Street—the urge to merge, to diversify, to capitalize on success"* as Paul Volcker put it in the Foreword to my *Confessions of a Municipal Bond Salesman*. I was present and accounted for when MBIA decided to capitalize on the success we had gilding the lily and building confidence in munis. Why not do the same thing for other businesses? We would start insuring collateralized debt obligations (CDOs) backed by pools of corporate bonds, mortgages, auto loans, credit cards, or even pubs. Next, we would sell credit default swaps (CDSs).

Even the sophisticated business press, trying to explain what CDSs are, throws up its hands up and describes them just as "risky, complicated financial instruments"—something akin to saying, "You don't want to know." Sure you do, and I'm going to tell you. A CDS is an insurance policy, for a given premium, guaranteeing to make up the loss in a security that defaults to an institution that may have guaranteed to make up the loss on that same security to another institution, that may have guaranteed to make up the loss on that same security to still another institution … and so on … none of the players betting that the security will or won't default required to own and have an "insurable interest" in the actual security in question. After all, how much exposure could there really be when one guy's bet that my house will burn down is netted against another guy's bet that it won't? Except for a deadbeat here, and a bankrupt there, net exposure within the universe of counterparties should be zero—in theory.

I am down to my fingertips a municipal bond salesman. I deal in an investment that has had an historic cumulative default rate, up to September 2008, of one-tenth of 1 percent for every municipal bond rated from top to bottom, from Aaa to C by Moody's, and three-tenths of 1 percent for every municipal bond rated AAA to C by Standard & Poor's. Municipalities can't simply pull up stakes whenever the going gets tough. Governments have to stay in business. Their debts remain. Losses are recoverable. How could the entire municipal bond insurance industry convince itself that its success with munis, which so rarely default, is interchangeable with mortgages and other businesses that can default, do, and did? By 2008, "triple-A, insured" had all the relevance of "no new taxes," and "he kept us out of war." CDOs and CDSs had dragged MBIA's stellar triple-As down to NR (non-rated) by Fitch, B3 by Moody's, and BBB+ by S&P, and brought the premier insurer of municipal bonds almost to its knees.

We forgot that it wasn't our insurance that made municipal bonds safe. Insurance simply made municipal bonds more marketable. Just the way insuring collateralized debt obligations and credit default swaps —and rating them triple-A—would make these enigmatic inventions marketable. Just think, if the rating agencies hadn't bestowed those triple-A blessings, Wall Street could never have palmed off more trillions of dollars of CDSs in volumes that would eventually exceed the sum of all the outstanding munis, Treasuries, federal agencies, and equities combined.

As we go to press, not only the municipal bond insurance companies but the whole world is unwinding, unleveraging, and writing down those "complicated, risky financial instruments." Nations are crawling out of the attendant wreckage. There's got to be a lesson in what the financial geniuses have brought down on the heads of innocent, risk-averse bystanders. Maybe it's to listen to your inner voice. It's not all that inner. If you can't explain an investment to yourself, it's the security's way of declaring, "I'm not for you." Get up from the meeting. Excuse yourself. Walk out to the lake. Get in the canoe. And paddle to a distant shore.

Postscript from The Bond Buyer, February 19, 2009:

"Following through on a transformation plan announced last year, MBIA Inc. yesterday said it has restructured its insurance subsidiaries to form a new U.S. public finance-only insurer that will operate separately from its structured finance business.

Bond insurance subsidiary MBIA Insurance Corp. ceded its entire $537 billion book of public finance business to subsidiary MBIA Insurance Corp. of Illinois, which MBIA expects to rename National Public Finance Guarantee Corp. and limit to writing only U.S. public finance business. MBIA has paid MBIA Illinois approximately $2.89 billion for reinsuring the public finance business and capitalized it with an additional $2.09 billion."

As of May 2009, National Public Finance Guarantee Corp. is non-rated (NR) by Fitch, Baa1 on Moody's "Positive Credit Watchlist" and AA- on S&P's "Developing Credit Watch."

11

Auction Rate Securities: The Risk that Wouldn't Go Away

THE HEADLINE, "Wall Street Lays An Egg," can't be used for the auction rate securities debacle, because *Variety*, the show business newspaper, already used laying an egg in 1929 to describe the Crash. But for magnificent understatement, it sure captures the grief and theatre of the absurd in the $330,000,000,000 frozen in auction rate securities—more than all the late pays in the Depression and New York City moratorium and the defaults of WPPSS and Orange County and the schemes of Arthur Abba Goldberg and Bernard Madoff, all combined.

Auction rate securities (ARS) were the creation of a star at the old Shearson Lehman with a genius for creating new securities out of common stocks and preferred perpetual shares with a maturity date of ... forever. His name is Ronald L. Gallatin. In 1984, Gallatin went to work on the age-old problem of how to make a liquid investment out of a perpetual, meaning, if you put a dollar in, you'll get a dollar out—when you want it.

Until then, a thirty-year bond meant you got your money back in thirty years, unless you sold it before maturity in the always-fluctuating open market. Gallatin's cure for "How much will I get if I have to sell my perpetual?" when applied by Goldman Sachs in 1988 to bonds, was a bond that would take the market risk off the back of principal and transfer it to the coupon rate. Every day, week, or month to stay abreast of current yields, the interest rate would be reset so that its current market value would always be par. The invention gave investors a new way to stay liquid, get in at par, get out at par, and earn a tax-free yield that kept abreast of short-term interest rates. Not only that, these ARS paid somewhat more than municipal money market funds and other short-term munis. They're called ARS for the most obvious of reasons. They are in a constant state of auction, weekly being the most common frequency. At its simplest, here's how these ARS work. At, say, 11 a.m. every Tuesday, if Tuesdays are the weekly interest reset day, buyers and any sellers who want to cash out are brought together electronically with a broker-dealer auctioneer. The buyers are actually bidding against each other for the sellers' securities—not in dollars, mind you (the dollar price will always be par), but in the *yield* each of the bidders is shooting for until the next auction and the next and the next … until the day the holders finally want out and put up their own ARS for auction.

Say these are the yields and amounts bid for $100,000,000 worth of ARS:

		Cumulative	"Clearing" Interest Rate Awarded
Amount	Bid		
$ 10,000,000	at 2.80%	= $10,000,000	3.20%
+ 20,000,000	at 2.90%	= $30,000,000	3.20%
+ 30,000,000	at 3.00%	= $60,000,000	3.20%
+ 30,000,000	at 3.10%	= $90,000,000	3.20%
+ 10,000,000	at 3.20%	= $100,000,000	3.20%
+ 10,000,000	at 3.30%	= $110,000,000	None

All the bidders required to speak up for the whole $100,000,000 at the lowest interest rate "clear the auction." In the example, all the bidders from 2.80 percent to 3.20 percent get the amount they bid for at the market clearing rate of 3.20 percent, even though there were only $10,000,000 bids at that level. The $10,000,000 bids at 3.30 percent get nothing.

It's the same "Dutch auction" mechanism they used to sell tulips in Holland in the sixteenth century, and the Treasury has been using for decades to price T-bills. Applied to munis, it sounded like an ideal setup. And it was just hunky-dory ... for twenty years, because:

1. The municipal securities were insured.

2. They were rated triple-A.

3. There was a ready supply of buyers.

4. But, if there weren't enough genuine bidders, the auctioneer was always ready to step in with a bid and take up the slack.

Suddenly, in 2004, the SEC sued fifteen banks and broker-dealers for manipulating clearing rates, favoring issuers over investors, favoring some investors over other investors, and failure to disclose that, in the absence of enough bids to clear the auction, the auctioneer would switch roles and become a bidder for its own inventory. Never mind that these very acts were the lubricant that enabled the ARS market to provide investors with liquidity, while also saving issuers money by letting them borrow at short-term interest rates. While neither affirming nor denying the accusation, the broker-dealers coughed up $13 million in fines. And the full disclosure that followed set the stage for an unnerved market.

In a sequence of toppling dominoes, beginning with falling home prices, the municipal bond insurance companies that had taken on billions of mortgage-backed securities were downgraded and ARS with them. Without those alluring triple-A ratings, bidders for the sellers' securities ran for the hills. And with their own write-downs and books to balance, the broker-dealer auctioneers could no longer afford to take up the slack. For all practical purposes, the ARS market was and is frozen.

Investors haven't exactly lost principal. They just can't get their hands on it, even though it is still drawing compensatory interest rates—up to 20 percent for a short while from the issuers of some failed ARS. Unfortunately, you can't leave the blunt fact out of the equation that investments in auction rate securities were made to set money aside to pay tuitions, close on business deals, pay off a mortgage, and for retirees to live on. Lives are on hold.

Scores of lawsuits (attorneys general of New York and Massachusetts among them) have resulted in Citibank, Merrill Lynch, Morgan Stanley, UBS, Wachovia, and others buying back tens of billions worth of ARS so far. It will take tens of billions of dollars more to unfreeze the liquid assets still stuck in the $330 billion ARS market, a debacle bigger than the defaults involved in the Great Depression, New York City moratorium, WPPSS, Orange County, and Abba Dabba Doo's caper, combined.

The Lebenthal lesson here is don't fool around with what a municipal bond is meant to be. It is what it is. It offers the glories of tax-free income and full return of your principal at maturity. But if you sell it between the day you buy it and the day it comes to maturity, you stand to make or lose money. Bonds go up. And bonds go down. Try to add liquidity to this equation (put a dollar in, get a dollar out any time you want it), and something's got to give. You simply shift market risk into some other corner of the risk paradigm. Ask the man who's sitting with frozen ARS. And I'll read you the "Rime of the Ancient Mariner": "Water, water, everywhere, nor any drop to drink."

12

"By Their Deeds You Shall Know Them."

WHAT WALL STREET has done with reckless abandon to the whole country's $14 trillion economy, Bernard Madoff has done to just $50 billion of it with premeditation and malice aforethought. No, I didn't know Bernie Madoff. But that it even occurs to me somebody might want to know of any connection I might have to the perpetrator of the scam of the ages is an acknowledgment of one thing we do have in common. We both have a family name on the company's door. The first thing I wondered when Madoff's colossal betrayal of trust hit the headlines was what the rub-off would be on the Lebenthal family municipal bond business that depends so heavily on trust? "Er—ah ... with all due respect, Mr. Lebenthal, and nothing personal intended," came the answer in the form of a question from my first visitor of the day. "What protection would I have from any rotten apples in your barrel?"

Since the Madoff affair, everyone has a valid license to fire at their financial adviser's feet and make him dance. For two hours that day, Campbell, as we shall call him, at first squirmed in the role of Spanish Inquisitor, and screwed up his courage to fire away with the stuff of due diligence that Madoff's clients could never quite muster. Campbell's questions are in italics. My answers are in regular type, edited and polished to make them more relevant to anybody else trying to size up the outfit they're thinking of dealing with. So, back to that first shot out of Campbell's gun:

If Madoff had been working for you, could he have gotten away with what he did?

No way can money be moved from one brokerage account to someone else's—even a spouse's—without the owner's instructions and authorization in writing, followed by the debiting of one account and crediting the other, which would then show up on both monthly statements. As for the bonds themselves, they're no longer in physical certificate form that someone could slip into a pocket under the cloak of night. They're now in book-entry-only form, blips in a giant computer at the Depository Trust Corporation (DTC). To tamper with them would require the complicity of both DTC and our clearing agent, Pershing Affiliate of the Bank of New York Mellon. I don't know about Madoff's private wealth management "hoo-hah" on the 17th floor of Manhattan's Lipstick Building. Our brokerage business is 99.99 percent record keeping under the scrutiny of the regulators at FINRA, who routinely inspect the paper trail for anything fishy and spring surprise visits on us. Unless I'm playing too dumb to steal, it boggles my imagination how Madoff did what he did to the tune of billions and got away with it for ten years. We wouldn't last until your next statement.

Yes, but things happen. What's my protection if something does go wrong because of a rotten apple in your barrel or, perish the thought, you go bankrupt?

Your account is protected by the Securities Investor Protection Corporation (SIPC) against the theft, conversion, misappropriation, or monetary loss resulting from the firm's financial failure for up to $500,000. Up to $100,000 of that can be in cash, the remainder in securities. Over and above that amount, you are protected with unlimited additional insurance against thievery, bankruptcy, foul play, up to the full value of the securities in your account. Understand, though, the protection is against our failure, not the bond market's failure as the result of falling prices or the issuer's default.

I give you my money. Do I get anything from you, even a piece of crinkly paper, to show I own that blip on the computer?

You get a confirmation in the mail describing what you bought— the name of issuer, coupon rate, maturity, call date and call price if the bond is callable, the price you paid, and the resulting yield to maturity, or to call, and accrued interest. And that confirmation is generated by our clearing agent, not in a back room by us. Hang onto it. That's your proof of ownership. You'll need it if you ever want to sell before maturity. You also get a statement from Pershing every month (quarterly, if there's no activity in the account), itemizing your holdings, showing current market values, activity (the movement of any cash or securities coming into the account or going out), interest paid in the current month, and any bonds in your portfolio that are coming due or being called next month.

How can I check on how much my bonds are worth between statements?

Your account with market values, updated daily, is accessible to you 24/7 by password on the Internet, as well as daily activity, announcement of any of your bonds that are going to be called, and news affecting the municipal bond market. You can also click and bring up a calendar of your projected interest payments coming in on the first and fifteenth of every month for one year ahead.

If something were to come up and I had to sell, what are the chances I'd actually receive the market value quoted on my monthly statement?

For a big block, a million or so, of an actively traded general market name? The evaluations are a close indication of what you'd actually receive. The evaluations are worked up on a grid system by firms, such as Kenny, Muller Data, and Mergent, that make a business of pricing municipal bonds using both real trades that actually took place and estimations of what other bonds of comparable rating, coupon, and maturity would be trading at. It's the direction of those evaluations from month to month—up or down—that indicates how you're doing. If you want to know exactly what your bonds are worth, call the house you bought them from or check around for a bid. That brings up my definition of marketability: the ability to get a bid from others than just the house you bought it from.

Let me ask you, will I do better buying municipal bonds from you? Are you cheaper?

There's nothing in needlepoint hanging on the walls around here saying "Be cheaper." I do believe that if another firm is offering the same bond—same issuer, coupon, and maturity at a lower price—if only you knew about it—then we ought to cut our price and match the other guy's and then try to compete on service and fit. But rather than my making a self-serving statement, let me ask you, what made you pick up the telephone? Why did you call us?

What's goes through your mind when you recommend a bond?

Same thing we look for in bidding on the bond for our inventory. Does it offer assuredness of interest? Safety of principal? Marketability? What's it worth in the current market? And who's going to buy it? We're going to own that bond until we find a customer for that particular coupon, maturity, and bond rating.

How do I know I'm paying a fair price?

Until your confidence is restored, you can log onto www. investinginbonds.com, and compare anybody's offering price, ours included, to the actual price being paid for the very same bond anywhere in the country. Just follow these steps. Under the header Municipal Price Data, click, in succession, the underlined instruction See Municipal Markets At-A-Glance, and next under Bond History enter the CUSIP number of the bond in question. Click CONTINUE, and a page describing the bond will come up. Click # OF TRADES, and voila! The real-time price of every trade in that identical bond, today and going back a few days, identified as either a Sale to Customer or Inter-dealer. Well, almost real-time. Every broker-dealer's clearing agent is hooked up to the Municipal Securities Rulemaking Board (MSRB) and has to report electronically all sales, retail and wholesale, within fifteen minutes of the trade. That means you can not only can compare price offerings to any real trades taking place in the retail market, but get an idea of how much the dealer paid and you might get paid if you turned right around and sold that bond right back.

How much are your commissions?

In lieu of charging commissions per se, we buy the bonds wholesale at the bid side of the market and sell them retail to you at the ask side. The spread between what we paid and charge you can range from $2.50 to $15.00 per thousand dollars of face value, depending on rating, maturity, activity of trading in that particular name, block size, and how long we think we'll have that bond before we can sell it.

I've got to know I can sell my bonds without taking a shellacking. Who's going to want to buy a bond from me of some one-horse town they've never heard of?

One-horse town? Now you've gone too far. Seriously, if it's a general obligation backed by the full faith, credit, unlimited taxing power, and all the other financial resources of the issuer, Lebenthal, for one, is going to buy them. They're our bread and butter. They're the blue chips of the bond business that have earned for all municipal bonds their reputation for safety. We want your Butternuts and Unadilla, New York, school district bonds, your Horseheads and Big Flats. It's not up to you to find the buyer. That's our job.

What's better? New issues or bonds that have been around and have come back into the market?

Theoretically, it should make no difference. When we bid on bonds, we take into account what's trading at what levels in the secondary market. And if new issues come to market at a lower or higher yield, we adjust our secondary offerings accordingly. Money is money. But if peace of mind to you is knowing that the price you're being asked to pay is the same price to one and all, then buy new issues. Put in your order during the "retail offering period," take your chances of its being filled, and getting bonds at the public offering price.

Who's Fulvio & Associates LLP?

Our auditors as well as the auditors to about 200 other broker-dealers, large and small.

How long have you been in business?

Not counting the eighty years and three generations of Lebenthals at the old Lebenthal & Co., Inc., which ceased to exist in 2005 when our company was acquired by Merrill Lynch, on March 1, 2009, the new Lebenthal & Co., LLC was one year old in the eyes of the regulators at FINRA. A year ago, Merrill Lynch sold us back our name for a song. My daughter Alexandra Lebenthal had already brought me out of retirement to join her selling municipal bonds at our new wealth management and family office firm, which she named Lebenthal & Co., LLC is now the retail and institutional munibond division of Alexandra & James, LLC.

13

Who Reads the Prospectus, Anyway?
(Hey, It's Only Your Money!)

SO YOU CAN'T bother buying an individual municipal bond, weighing ratings, balancing yield against maturity, and all that? Then why not log onto the Internet and download a prospectus for a mutual fund of municipal bonds as the first step in reaching for yield and spreading the risk over a whole portfolio of municipal bonds? A prospectus. You know, as in the ubiquitous tagline from the commercials: "Send for a free prospectus containing more complete information, including all sales charges, risks, fees, and taxes. Read carefully *before you invest!*"

But, come on! How many mutual fund shareholders ever read the prospectus? Not you, I'll bet. The impenetrable length of some of those hundred-pagers seems almost designed to keep you in ignorant bliss. Well, starting in 2009, you won't have that excuse anymore. New SEC regulations will permit a clear, concise "plain-English" summary prospectus to fulfill a fund's prospectus delivery obligation, as long as the fund still makes the real McCoy available on the Internet.

Maybe this will grab your interest. Here are eight information nuggets from mutual fund prospectuses downloaded on the Internet. At the end of each one, I have tacked on a little quiz to see how disclosure squares with you? Simply check which facial expression comes closest to how you feel about what you've read. Add up the smiles, the frowns, the blank expressions, and then decide. What'll it be? Individual bonds? Funds of bonds? But, if you're of the Lebenthal school of deciding, "Yes …" or "No!" and it's neither, remember: it's always okay to say, "Thanks a lot, Jim—but, no thanks. I'm keeping my money in the bank."

1. Total Return

The fund earns interest, dividends, and other income from its investments and distributes this income (less expenses) to shareholders as dividends. The fund also realizes capital gains from its investments and distributes these gains (less any losses) to shareholders as capital gain distributions.

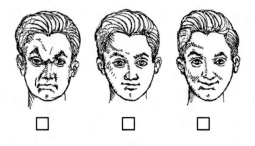

2. Fees

Fees and expenses reduce the investment performance of a portfolio. Some of these fees are paid directly by you at the time of investment (for example, a front-end sales charge) or, under certain circumstances, at the time you redeem or sell your shares back to a portfolio. You pay other fees and expenses indirectly because they are deducted from a portfolio's assets and reduce the value of your shares. These fees include management fees, distribution and/or service (Rule 12b-1) fees, and operating expenses.

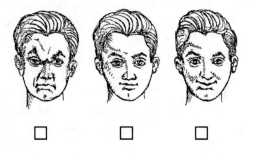

3. Seeking performance

The adviser may increase its allocation to noninvestment-grade securities without limitation. The adviser may invest up to 100 percent of the fund's assets in noninvestment-grade, tax-exempt securities. The fund also may invest in tax-exempt securities that are trading at a price less than the original issue price (or market discount bonds), enter into credit default swap arrangements and other derivative transactions, and engage in other permissible activities that will likely cause the fund to realize a limited amount of ordinary income or short-term capital gains (which are treated as ordinary income for federal income tax purposes) and, as a result, may result in taxable distributions to shareholders. The ordinary income derived from these investment strategies generally will be limited to approximately 5 percent or less of the fund's annual distributions. The fund may use derivative contracts or hybrid instruments to increase or decrease the portfolio's exposure to the investment(s) underlying the derivative or hybrid. Additionally, by way of example, the fund may use derivative contracts in an attempt to:

- increase or decrease the effective duration of the fund portfolio;

- obtain premiums from the sale of derivative contracts;

- realize gains from trading a derivative contract; or

- hedge against potential losses.

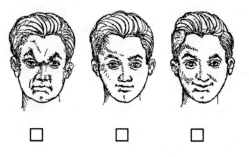

4. Risks

An investment in the fund could lose money over short or even long periods. You should expect the fund's share price and total return to fluctuate within a wide range, like the fluctuations of the overall bond market. The fund's performance could be hurt by:

• *State-specific risk,* because the fund invests primarily in securities issued by California and its municipalities, it is more vulnerable to unfavorable developments in California than are funds that invest in municipal securities of many states.

• *Interest rate risk,* which is the chance that bond prices overall will decline because of rising interest rates. Interest rate risk should be high for the fund because it invests mainly in long-term bonds, whose prices are much more sensitive to interest rate changes than are the prices of short-term bonds.

• *Call risk,* which is the chance that during periods of falling interest rates, issuers of callable bonds may call (repay) securities with higher coupons or interest rates before their maturity dates. The fund would then lose potential price appreciation and would be forced to reinvest the unanticipated proceeds at lower interest rates, resulting in a decline in the fund's income. Call risk is generally high for long-term bond funds.

• *Credit risk,* which is the chance that a bond issuer will fail to pay interest and principal in a timely manner, or that negative perceptions of the issuer's ability to make such payments will cause the price of that bond to decline.

• *Municipal market risk.* Factors include political or legislative changes and uncertainties related to the tax status of municipal securities or investor rights. The value of municipal bonds is strongly influenced by the value of tax-exempt income to investors. A significant restructuring of federal income taxes, or even serious discussion on this topic in Congress, could cause municipal bond prices to fall, as lower income tax rates would reduce the advantage of owning municipals. The yield and value of a portfolio's investments in municipal securities is vulnerable to the perception that one issuer's difficulties could affect them all.

• *Nondiversification risk,* which is the chance that the fund's performance may be hurt disproportionately by the poor performance of relatively few securities. The fund is considered nondiversified, which means that it may invest a greater percentage of its assets in the securities of particular issuers as compared with other mutual funds.

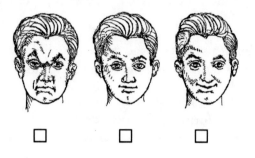

5. Derivatives

Each fund may invest in derivatives. In general, derivatives may involve risks different from, and possibly greater than, those of the underlying securities, assets, or market indexes. Generally speaking, a derivative is a financial contract whose value is based on the value of a financial asset, a physical asset, or a market index. The fund may invest in derivatives only if the expected risks and rewards of the derivatives are consistent with the investment objective, policies, strategies, and risks of the fund as disclosed in this prospectus.

The fund's derivative investments may include fixed-income futures contracts, fixed-income options, interest rate swaps, total return swaps, credit default swaps, or other derivatives. Investments in derivatives can involve leverage. Leverage has the effect of magnifying returns, positively or negatively ... Losses (or gains) involving futures contracts can sometimes be substantial—in part because a relatively small price movement in a futures contract may result in an immediate and substantial loss (or gain) for a fund.

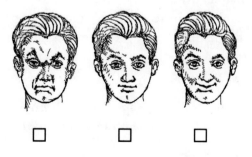

6. Taxes

• Regular monthly dividends (including those from the state-specific tax-free funds) are expected to be exempt from federal income taxes.

• Exemption is not guaranteed, since the fund has the right under certain conditions to invest in nonexempt securities.

• You must report your total tax-free income on IRS Form 1040. The IRS uses this information to help determine the tax status of any Social Security payments you may have received during the year.

• For state-specific funds, the monthly dividends you receive are expected to be exempt from state and local income tax of that particular state. For other funds, a small portion of your income dividend may be exempt from state and local income taxes.

• If the funds invest in certain "private activity" bonds, shareholders who are subject to the alternative minimum tax (AMT) must include income generated by those bonds in their AMT calculation. The portion of the fund's income dividend that should be included in your AMT calculation, if any, will be reported to you in January on Form 1099-INT.

• Gains realized on the sale of market discount bonds with maturities beyond one year may be treated as ordinary income and cannot be offset by other capital losses.

• "Market discount" bonds can cause the fund to recognize ordinary income. Market discount is a discount at which a bond is purchased that is attributable to a decline in the value of the bond after its original issuance. The market discount is then taken into account ratably over the bond's remaining term to maturity, and the portion that accrues during the fund's holding period, for the bond is generally treated as taxable ordinary income to the extent of any realized gain on the bond on disposition or maturity.

• Payments received or gains realized on certain derivative transactions may result in taxable ordinary income or capital gain.

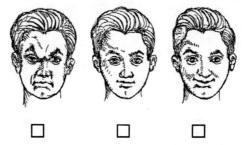

7. Turnover

Turnover is an indication of frequency of trading. We will not generally trade in securities for short-term profits, but when circumstances warrant, securities may be purchased and sold without regard to the length of time held. Each time the fund purchases or sells a security, it incurs a cost. This cost is reflected in the fund's net asset value but not in its operating expenses. The higher the turnover rate, the higher the transaction costs and the greater the impact on the fund's total return. Higher turnover can also increase the possibility of taxable capital gain distributions.

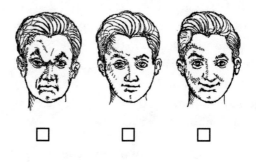

8. NAV

The fund's net asset value per share (NAV) is the value of a single share. To calculate NAV, a portfolio's assets are valued and totaled, liabilities are subtracted, and the balance, called net assets, is divided by the number of shares outstanding. The fund's assets are valued primarily on the basis of information furnished by a pricing service or market quotations. If market quotations or information furnished by a pricing service is not readily available or does not accurately reflect fair value for a security, or if a security's value has been materially affected by events occurring before the fund's pricing time but after the close of the market on which the security is principally traded, such securities may be valued by the board of trustees or its delegate at fair value. Due to the subjective and variable nature of fair value, it is possible that the fair value determined for a particular security may be different from the value realized on sale of the security.

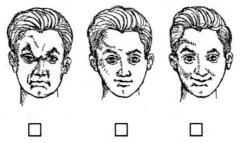

In the light of what you've just read, go back to the discussion in Chapter 8. Should you build your own portfolio or hire a manager to build one for you?

You'd expect me to prefer the little nuances of picking and choosing individual bonds, weighing their ratings, balancing yield against maturity, and all that. But an investor has to have a certain amount of money to spread around and do the picking and choosing that a mutual fund manager can do for you, whether it's for $10,000, $100,000, or $1,000,000. Besides diversification, there is one other thing I can't do with my individual bonds that a fund can: reinvest monthly or quarterly dividends automatically so that tax-free interest earns more interest, builds and rebuilds on itself.

I take that back. I work very nicely reinvesting the proceeds of a portfolio of size. A portfolio of $5,000,000 in individual municipal bonds at 5 percent spins off $250,000 a year—enough to build a ladder of five fifty-bond blocks, going out five years. Such is the blessing of working with big numbers.

14

How to Slow Down a Fast-Talking Bond Salesman

ASK that salesperson to send you an Official Statement (OS). It's the issuer's public-offering document, disclosing everything you could conceivably want to know about a new issue of municipal bonds that a cold caller might not bother to mention in the exuberance of dialing for dollars:

- who the issuer is, amount being borrowed, and what the money is for

- the security behind the bonds

- maturities, coupon rates, and call features

- ratings

- where the bondholder stands in line when it comes to getting paid

- how the issuer is doing financially

- tax collections if it's a GO, earnings if it's a revenue bond

- debt service coverage

- rate covenants pegging taxes or user charges to meet debt service requirements

- outstanding debt hanging over the issuer's head

- tax status

- litigation

Between the roman-numbered, arabic-numbered, and letter-numbered pages, there's enough information in an OS to pull the rug out from any unsubstantiated claim. Running off at the mouth can happen in selling. As a case in point, by now you may have figured, the New York City subways are my poster child for promoting the good that municipal bonds do. The MTA ought to put up a sign somewhere: Built By Bonds.

The MTA operates the largest transit and commuter rail system in all of North America. Every day, the MTA handles 8 million trips on its subways, rails, and buses. The seven bridges and two tunnels service 900,000 vehicles per day. Over 2,000 miles of track and 700 stations as well as 5,800 buses and 8,500 rail cars are maintained by the MTA.

I underwrite, recommend, and sell MTAs. I have advertised MTA bonds on TV ("My job's easy. All I have to do is make you love the subway and the tax-free bonds I sell that built them." "Do I take the subway? Of course, I do. I'm a New Yorker.") I'll bet, in the blood rush of selling MTAs, I've actually said some of the stuff I'm now going to do my best to dig up from memory. Just for the record, here's what the OS for MTA Transportation Revenue Bonds, Series 2008C also has to say on the same subjects, officially.

JIM L: Those are workers going to jobs in the morning and paychecks going home to the neighborhoods at night.

OS: MTA has responsibility for developing and implementing a single, integrated mass transportation policy for MTA's service region (the MTA Commuter Transportation District), which consists of New York City and the seven New York metropolitan-area counties of Dutchess, Nassau, Orange, Putnam, Rockland, Suffolk, and Westchester. It carries out some of those responsibilities by operating the Transit and Commuter Systems through its subsidiary and affiliate entities: the New York City Transit Authority and its subsidiary, the Manhattan and Bronx Surface Transit Operating Authority; the Staten Island Rapid Transit Operating Authority; The Long Island Rail Road Company; the Metro-North Commuter Railroad Company; the Metropolitan Suburban Bus Authority (MTA Long Island Bus); the MTA Bus Company; and MTA Capital Construction Company.

JIM L: At A2 by Moody's, MTA Transportation Bonds are investment grade, albeit at the lower end of the investment grade spectrum.

OS: Three major items worsened for the two-year period 2008 and 2009:

Fuel and Energy Costs: These projected costs are expected to be worse than forecast in the February Plan by $208 million over the two year period, a 39% increase; these costs are projected to increase by $81 million in 2008 and $127 million in 2009. The out years are also projected to worsen by $66 million in 2010 and $60 million in 2011. The Plan reflects Global Insight projections as of June 2008, which assume that prices will peak during the second half of 2009 and decline slightly thereafter.

Real Estate Tax Revenues: The falling real estate market in the region, notably the sharp downturn in City commercial real estate activity, is projected to result in $443 million in lower revenues for the two year period; $201 million in 2008 and $242 million in 2009. The Plan assumes that these revenues will remain in a decline during 2010 and 2011 and begin to grow in 2012. These projections are consistent with the City's Executive Budget.

State Taxes: Appropriation for MTA … was $37 million lower than expected in the 2008 Adopted Budget. This reduction resulted from late Statewide reductions of aid to localities. The State's projections issued with the Enacted Budget for taxes supporting MTTF Receipts and MMTOA Receipts (each defined below) are projected to negatively impact MTA by $60 million for the two-years, 2008 and 2009, compared with the February Plan. The State's projections for these taxes are forecast to worsen MTA's revenues by $84 million in 2010 and $121 million in 2011.

JIM L: Because the city comes to a screeching halt without mass transit, MTA's Transportation Bonds have two things going for them: essentiality and revenues coming every which-what way.

OS: Sources of Payment. Pledged Transportation Pledged Revenues

- MTA receives "transportation revenues" directly and through certain subsidiaries (currently, MTA Long Island Rail Road, MTA Metro-North Railroad, and MTA bus) and affiliates (currently MTA New York City Transit and MaBSTOA) …

- MTA Bridges and Tunnels is required by law to transfer its annual operating surpluses … to MTA …

- MTA receives subsidies for transit from the State and matching subsidies from New York City, and … for commuter from the State and matching subsidies from New York City and the seven counties in the MTA district …

- Non-operating revenue from the "Urban Tax" collection … and Excess Mortgage Recording Taxes …

- MTA receives subsidies from … taxes imposed on petroleum business (PBT), motor fuel taxes on gasoline and diesel fuel, and certain motor vehicle fees administered by the State Department of Motor Vehicles, including both registration and non-registration fees …

- the sales and compensating use tax within the MTA transportation district,

- two franchise taxes imposed on certain transportation and transmission companies, and

- a temporary surcharge on a portion of the franchise tax imposed on certain corporations, banks, insurance, utility, and transportation companies attributable to business activities within the transportation district

- MTA is reimbursed by the City and the seven counties in the MTA district ... for the cost of staffing the stations, maintaining the stations and appurtenant land and buildings ... in addition the City provides the policing of the Transit System

- MTA earns income, as do its subsidiaries and affiliates, from the temporary investment of money held in those of MTA's various funds and accounts that are pledged to holders of Transportation Revenue Obligation.

- Other ... advertising and concession revenues.

JIM L: Debt service in 2007 was $681 million. Revenues available for debt service were $8.502 billion. Name me one other bond with 12.4 times coverage.

OS:

TABLE 2
(In $ Millions)
Summary of Pledged Revenues
(Calculated in Accordance with the Transportation Resolution) and Expenses
Historical Cash Basis (in Millions)

			2007
Revenues from Systems Operations			
	Fares from Transit System	$ 2,857	
	Fares from Commuter System	956	
	Fares from MTA Bus	160	
	Other Income	210	
Sub-Total—Operating Revenues			4,183

Revenues from MTA Bridges/Tunnels Surplus		406	
Revenues from Governmental Sources			
	State/Local Gen'l Operating Subsidies	396	
	Special Tax Supp'ted Operating Subsidies		
	DTF Excess	363	
	MMTOA Receipts	1,576	
	Urban Tax	883	
	Excess Mtg Recording Taxes	<u>27</u>	
Sub-Total Special Tax-Supp'ted OpSubsidies		2,849	
Station Maintenance/Service Reimbursements		410	
City Subsidy for MTA Bus		187	
Rev from Investment of Cap Program Funds		<u>71</u>	
Sub-Total—Non Operating Revenues			4,319
TOTAL TRANSPORTATION RESOLUTION PLEDGED REVENUES			**$ 8,502**
BUDGETED DEBT SERVICE			**$ 681**
Transit Operating Expenses		5,454	
Commuter Operating Expenses		1,954	
MTA Bus Operating Expenses		<u>387</u>	
Other Expenses of Related Entities			
Total Operating Expenses			**$ 7,795**
Total Operating Expenses and Debt Service			**$ 8,476**

Based on the MTA 2009 Preliminary Budget and July 2009-2012 Financial Plan presented to the MTA Board on July 23, 2008

JIM L: Transportation bondholders get paid ahead of subway workers, ahead of maintenance, ahead of operations … you name it.

OS: Holders of Transportation Revenue Bonds are to be paid prior to the payment, from pledged revenues, of operating or other expenses of MTA, MTA New York City Transit, MaBSTOA, MTA Long Island Rail Road, MTA Metro-North Railroad, and MTA Bus. However, MTA's ability to generate major portions of the pledged revenues depends upon its payment of operating and other expenses.

JIM L: MTA does not have to run to New York State or New York City for their approval to raise fares. If MTA must raise fares to pay bondholders, it must.

OS: The level of fare revenues depends to a large extent on MTA's ability to maintain and/or increase ridership levels on the Transit, Commuter, and MTA Bus Systems … Considering the impact of increased fares on riders and on the regional economy, MTA's policy is to attempt to reduce costs or obtain additional revenues from other sources, mainly governmental sources, before increasing fares. As a result, even though MTA does not generally need other governmental approvals before setting fares, the amount and timing of fare increases may be affected by the Federal, State, and local government financial conditions, as well as by budgetary and legislative processes …

Ability to Comply with Rate Covenant and Pay Operating and Maintenance Expenses. The Transit, Commuter, and MTA Bus Systems have depended, and are expected to continue to depend, upon government subsidies to meet capital and operating needs. Thus, even though MTA is legally obligated by the rate covenant to raise fares sufficiently to cover all capital and operating costs, there can be no assurance that there is any level at which Transit, Commuter, and MTA Bus Systems fares would produce revenues sufficient to comply with the rate covenant, particularly if the current level (or the assumed level in the budgets prepared in connection with 2008 and the forecasts prepared in connection with 2009 through 2012) of collection of dedicated taxes, operating subsidies, and expense reimbursements were to be discontinued or substantially reduced.

JIM L: I'm not asking you to take the subway. I'm asking you to take the MTA's money.

OS: Hawkins Delafield & Wood LLP is Bond Counsel for the Series 2008C Bonds. Their opinion under existing law, relying on certain statements by MTA and assuming compliance by MTA with certain covenants, is that interest on the Series 2008C Bonds is:

☐ excluded from a bondholder's federal gross income under the Internal Revenue Code of 1986,

☐ not a preference item for a bondholder under the federal alternative minimum tax, and

☐ included in the adjusted current earnings of a corporation under the federal corporate alternative minimum tax.

The point of putting myself down as one of those "Have I Got a Bond For You" characters is to point up the OS as the ultimate tranquilizer gun for the fast-talking bond salesman. The OS is not meant to sell. It's meant to tell. And we municipal securities dealers are required to deliver to you, "no later than the settlement date of the transaction a copy of an official statement in preliminary form," and in final form no later than the business day following its receipt by us. An OS can run well over a hundred pages. I used to joke, "I'll give you a dollar for every page you read, if you'll give me a dollar for every page you don't." Until the current economic crisis hit, and money turned out to be not so funny.

15

To the New Kid in Sales
(And Talking To Investors Over the New Kid's Shoulder)

Look what they've done to my song, Ma

Look what they've done to my song, Ma

Well they tied it up in a plastic bag

And turned it upside down, Ma

Look what they've done to my song

"What Have They Done to My Song, Ma?"

Words and Music by Melanie Safka

Copyright © 1970 by Kama Rippa Music Inc. and Amelanie Music, Copyright Renewed. All Rights for the World Assigned to Bienstock Publishing Co. and Quartet Music. International Copyright Secured. All Rights Reserved. Used by Permission.

It's not your ma's municipal bond market anymore, son. Look what this boilerplate from a typical municipal bond fund prospectus has done to her song: "They've tied it up in a plastic bag and turned it upside down."

A Portfolio may use derivatives to earn income and enhance return, to hedge or adjust the risk profile of a portfolio, to replace more traditional direct investments and to obtain exposure to otherwise inaccessible markets.

A Portfolio's use of derivatives may involve risks that are different from, or possibly greater than, the risk associated with investing directly in securities or other more traditional instruments. These risks include the risk that the value of a derivative instrument may not correlate perfectly, or at all, with the value of the assets, reference rates, or indices that they are designed to track. Other risks include the possible absence of a liquid secondary market for a particular instrument and possible exchange-imposed price fluctuation limits, either of which may make it difficult or impossible to close out a position when desired; the risk that adverse price movements in an instrument can result in a loss substantially greater than the Portfolio's initial investment in that instrument (in some cases, the potential loss is unlimited); and the risk that the counterparty will not perform in its obligations.

The derivatives referred to—swaps, swaptions, inverse floaters, and synthetics— have turned fixed-rate, long-term, buy-to-hold munis into Tender Option Bonds, Auction Rate Securities, and leveraged interest rate plays that overhang the market. When margins get called and the leverage unwinds, a glut of supply comes screaming back, driving up borrowing costs just when our cities and towns are trying to issue bonds for public necessities. It's not the municipal bond business I learned at the knee of my mother Sayra Lebenthal, the founder's, when she fired me with conviction:

Munis are the rock bed foundation of our roads and runways, subways and sewers, schools and bridges.

Our cities and states can afford to borrow without diluting ability to pay as long as they borrow for productive investments that pay for themselves in long-term economic growth.

Infrastructure is capital that creates more capital. You plant it. It grows. And gives you more seed corn to plant anew.

Belief is the conviction you bring to the thing you're selling. Belief gives you an owner's stake in the product. Let me give you an example of where believing can lead. Back in the old days, the states couldn't tax the interest of federal securities, and the federal government couldn't tax the municipal bonds of the states. "That's reciprocal tax immunity, Son," as Mother explained it. But then, Congress went and passed the tax on Social Security benefits in 1983, a new law that made retirees include the tax-free interest from their munis when computing the tax on their Social Security benefits. What was I to do? Sit back and let the feds call Mother a liar? Not me. So I tracked down Louis and Mary Boli of Santa Barbara, California, who, except for their "tax-free" municipal bonds, would have owed no tax on their Social Security benefits. I got Lebenthal to bankroll Boli v. Baker (James Baker, Ronald Reagan's secretary of treasury), suing to have the Social Security tax ruled unconstitutional. Well, we lost that one—but conviction conferred authority to what I was selling. And ever after those were *my* bonds, *my* subways, and *my* sewers I was fighting for.

What could have made a guy with the dullest, squarest profession in America think his *Confessions of a Municipal Bond Salesman* would be worth reading. Well, possibly because I ran a successful bond business with only half a brain. The *right* half, the intuitive half that creative ideas come from, the half that I flew by the seat of my pants with, the half that turned municipal bonds into Lebenthal's workhorse, Lebenthal's cash cow, Lebenthal's babies.

If only I had waited three years. Today I'd really have something powerful to confess—my outrage. At an industry, my industry, that was doing just fine for itself and for the whole country, financing the infrastructure and raising the money to pay for the physical underpinnings of our increasingly good life. But then, felled by the curse of good times, we lost our sense of purpose. We made a lousy decision: let's turn munis into highly leveraged derivatives that would defy gravity and return 10 percent, 11 percent, 12 percent tax free in a 4 ½ percent market. Let's make them auction rate securities that would go on forever and ever, taking thirty-year bonds and turning them into seven-day "cash equivalents," until one dark day no bidders showed up and the auctions failed. Let's take the risk out of risk—collateralize it, securitize it, slice it, dice it—atomize it—make it so small we can insure it, rate it triple-A and blacktop the globe with it.

Kid, after the way financial markets have wrecked our $14 trillion economy and what Bernie Madoff did to an eye-popping $50 billion of it, all by himself, investors have every right to be wary of us. Well, a piece of advice: never say, "Trust me!" Because, like charity, deeds have to speak for themselves. On the upbeat, positive, bright side, the existence of $2.7 trillion of municipal bonds is a feather in the cap of our better selves and a plus for the American dream. In her book *Reviving the American Dream,* the economist Alice Rivlin, who was the first woman director of the Office of Management and Budget under Bill Clinton, talks about the "surge" in the nation's output between 1940 and 1973 that "made it possible for almost everybody to live better and for the nation to improve both its public and its private capital at the same time."

For me, that dream of betterment—each generation doing better than the previous one—was caught up by Life Magazine in 1950 in this shot of Darwin Smith, a Ford autoworker, and his family standing in front of their own home ... TV antenna on the roof ... Ford Fairlane in the driveway. Nice car. I mean the pedal car Darwin Jr. is sitting in. You ever notice how kids in snapshots in the '50s always looked dressed up for Easter?

JUN MIKI, LIFE MAGAZINE © TIME WARNER INC

Detroit auto worker's family in 1950s

Nowadays, you go to the Gap and Banana Republic for torn jeans—torn jeans, a sign of what a lot of kids expect from the American Dream.

Once upon a time, on an airplane, a lovely lady sitting next to me asked what I did? I told her I was a municipal bond salesman. She said, "No. That's what you are. But what do you do?" "Well, if you put it that way, I dig roads, build schools, lay sewers, bore tunnels, bridge rivers, pave runways, and raise the money for most of the public works in America." "No kidding," she said, "How'd you get a job like that?"

Don't you choke on that word "infrastructure?" The way it sticks to the roof of the mouth like peanut butter on white bread? But tell the truth. When you contemplate those ribbons of concrete and steel leaping over rivers and obstacles to traffic and commerce ... and the subways you love to hate, moving us to work on time and home again ... and the pastel-clad structures that disguise incinerators that rid us of our leftovers in this land of plenty, recycling waste back into useful form, aren't you wowed by what Man, builder, digger, tunneler, reacher for the moon can do?

Look for the "yield implicit in the project." I don't mean just the immediate construction jobs and the tin in people's jeans from coupons spinning off all that tax-free interest every six months. I'm talking about the long-lasting benefits from infrastructure for generations to come. Write down this formula on a tablecloth. It'll make you famous one day.

Investment in infrastructure equals improved productivity equals higher standards of living equals better quality of life.

I'll tell you what I mean. Early on, Lebenthal promoted tax-free minibonds, so the average workingman and workingwoman could buy them for just 1,000 bucks. Our subway ads shouted in eye-grabbing type, "Put $1,000 in. Take $2,000 out. And pay no tax!" One day a guy called, "Lebenthal! I saw your ad," he said. "'Put $1,000 in? Take $2,000 out. Pay no tax?' One question, where the hell do I get the thousand?"

Where? From another guy's thousand, invested in better tools of production that give rise to more jobs, more paychecks, and more savings for everybody—including for the guy who called and asked, "Where do I get the thousand?"

The yield implicit in the project is simply everything you get back from public investment in public works that flows down to the bottom line as quality of life!

To simplify it you gotta believe, but don't kid yourself. Local governments have a strong incentive to generate the taxes or revenues to pay debt service—in full and on time—for the day down the road when even sovereigns have to go back to their creditors hat in hand. But the fact is that in the Depression, the failure of individual homeowners to meet their tax bills on time caused financial shortages in a number of municipalities and the late payment of 15 percent of the debt that was due between 1929 and 1937. And in our time we've had the moratorium, WPPSS, Orange County, and now Jefferson County. Better the bad news come from you than a refractory customer who knows just enough to leave you with egg on your face. If it's knowable, make sure the customer knows it. If it isn't, don't pretend.

Believe in debt, not deficit.

The "yield implicit in the project."

Capital that creates more capital.

Commitment to pay.

Preservation of credit.

Tax exemption that saves our cities and towns money when they borrow, as well as saving investors money in the taxes forgone when they lend.

And the beauty of the fixed-income investment in this age of anxiety, with its yield to maturity that's knowable and quotable up front.

You also better understand the human race, what people with money need and the games they play. And, oh yes. Risk! Ain't it awful? For every positive about a bond you recommend, you have to identify the risks, the reasons the bond might not be suitable for that particular individual: credit risk (likelihood of default), market risk (perceptions of deteriorating creditworthiness on resale price), interest rate risk (impact of fluctuating interest rates throughout the economy on market value of outstanding bonds), callability risk, taxability risk. And you have to stop the client in his tracks when he makes false assumptions about safety, tax exemption, and other poppycock like, "Uncle Sam will never let the city go down."

Make the broker's Obligation of Disclosure from the NASD's Rule Of Fair Practice your own standard for disclosing the risks and helping investors decide, "Yes … " or "No!" And you will be doing the most responsible and honest job you'll ever perform as a broker:

> A broker has a duty to disclose all material information in connection with an investment recommendation … which may be reasonably relevant to an investor to take into consideration in making an informed investment decision… in particular the various risks and level of risk of an investment recommendation.

Own it, and you'll never have to speak the sniveling words "trust me." Your deeds will speak for themselves.

16

Munis Doing Just Swimmingly In Waste-Water Treatment Plant Cleaning Up Our Rivers and Streams

"Crumbling," "structurally deficient," "functionally obsolete ..."

THEY MUST BE talking about infrastructure again. Every time a bridge collapses or a dam breaks, "crumbling infrastructure," "structurally deficient bridges," and "functionally obsolete *whatever*" leap to the tip of the tongue. Join the public outcry to rebuild America because more than the infrastructure has crumbled. The whole economy is in the tank. And yet, with all the talk about priming the pump and jump-starting the economy, you don't hear too much about the one tool our governors and mayors have for rebuilding America: munis, the lowly workhorse of investments. Instead, we're looking to TARP (the Troubled Asset Relief Program) and TALF (the Term Asset-Backed Securities Loan Facilities) and Uncle Sam's trillions to get this magnificent country off its magnificent bottom. The administration's $787 billion stimulus package has indeed allocated $27 billion to highway infrastructure investment, $8.4 billion to transit capital, $4 billion to clean water and $2 billion to drinking water state revolving funds (SRFs). That's all of $41 billion out of the whole $787 billion. I can't believe that here I am, belittling $41,000,000,000. Forty-one billion is a king's ransom in the context of the Founding Father's disdain for the federal government being in the business of building roads and facilitating "internal improvements," as they called infrastructure in those days.

Even though some of the grandest public works in America—the Transcontinental Railroad, Boulder and Grand Coulee Dams, TVA, and the Interstate Highway System—were built by the federal government, from the beginning of the Republic, there was never too much enthusiasm for socking federal taxpayers with the costs of internal improvements. In persuading the states to ratify the Constitution, James Madison took the position that transportation infrastructure would be the affair of the states. In 1830, Andrew Jackson vetoed federal funding of the Maysville Road in Kentucky, which would begin in Kentucky and end in Kentucky, as government waste, favoritism, and unfair to the rest of the country.

Die-hard free marketers still carp about how much good those thousands upon thousands of federal water and sewer systems, hospitals, schools, street, and highway projects built by the PWA and WPA did to pull us out of the Depression. Just in my own hometown, New York City's Triborough Bridge, Lincoln Tunnel, Queens Midtown Tunnel, Gowanus Expressway, Henry Hudson, Grand Central, Cross Island, and Interborough Parkways—even the electrification of the Pennsylvania Railroad from New York to Washington—were all financed with PWA loans. Wouldn't it be awful if you could never quite quantify the good from public investment in infrastructure, because it flows right down to the bottom line as quality of life? You be the judge whether nature ran its course and we just worked our way out of the Depression, or if those New Deal "boondoggles" unseized the economy and goosed the system. What's odd to me is that now, when the country has the chance of a lifetime to rebuild America, the distracted and conflicted municipal bond industry is out to lunch. Well, almost.

To me, the $4 billion and $2 billion in the Obama stimulus program allocated to SRFs and drinking water is a happy sign. Uncle Sam doesn't have to get all twisted into a pretzel doing the states' traditional job of digging roads, building schools, putting up hospitals, paving runways, moving commuters, boring tunnels, and bridging rivers. He's already invented the wheel. And it's right under his nose: those SRFs that, for two decades, funded 80 percent with federal money and 20 percent with state money, have been overhauling and retrofitting our wastewater treatment plants. The SRFs should be extended beyond their noble green purpose of improving our drinking water and cleaning up our rivers and streams to roads, to transportation, to restoring our infrastructure to at least a state of "good repair" in this land of milk and honey.

BLUEPRINT FOR AMERICA

Money raised by EFC bond sale is loaned out to governmental borrowers who issue their own G.O. bonds to EFC (or revenue bonds in case of NYC MuniWater) and receive an interest rate subsidy from earnings in the SRF.

At least one-third of the money to repay EFC is already on hand in the State Revolving Fund. The SRF is funded 80% by the federal government and 20% by matching New York State monies.

Local government borrowers issue their own general obligation or revenue bonds matched to repayment on EFC obligations and receive a below market interest rate which is subsidized from interest earnings on reserves.

State aid withheld from any municipality missing a debt service payment.

BOND OF THE DAY

$100,000,000 NYS EFC STATE REVOLVING FUND

Rated Aaa by Moody's, AAA by S&P, AAA by Fitch

LEBENTHAL

As individual loan is repaid, matching reserve requirement of borrower flows back into SRF to secure bonds of other borrowers—resulting in two to three times more monies available for other projects.

Exceptionally well secured...SRF collateralized by US governments and agencies...Triple-A by all three rating agencies: Moody's, S & P's and Fitch.

The SRF mechanism works like this. A state issues tax-free municipal bonds and lends the money to its cities and towns. The bonds are secured by the taxing power or revenue-generating power of the local borrower *plus* the cold, hard cash on reserve in the SRF. As the town pays back its loan, the reserves are used to secure new loans. Hence, the name State *Revolving* Fund. The process is going swimmingly, in fact so well that most of the various states' environmental facilities SRF bonds are rated triple-A by Fitch, Moody's, and Standard & Poor's, standing on their own two feet without third-party credit enhancements.

The amount being tossed around required to meet the country's infrastructure needs is in the trillions of dollars. With Treasury to the rescue of the economy and already on the hook for trillions (and counting), a ratio of 80 percent federal funding to seed an SRF for infrastructure—and only 20 percent from the states may be asking too much from the federal partner. But, if the federal government will pick up more of the states' share of Medicaid (22 percent of New York's budget) we, the states, could go somewhere closer to half to fund it and rebuild America with tax-free municipal bonds. Subject to a few conditions to make certain munis are up to the job:

1. Wonks, quants, and math geniuses need not apply. No using leverage. No borrowing short to carry long. No using municipal bonds as just another interest rate play. If Pennsylvania governor Ed Rendell and New York City mayor Mike Bloomberg are right about the country's unmet infrastructure needs (they say it's $1.6 trillion to bring the ailing infrastructure up to good repair; the American Society of Civil Engineers says it's more like $2.2 trillion over the next five years—and that's on top of the $2.7 trillion munis already outstanding), there's just too much at stake to play around. Munis are everybody's business, not just the private preserve of the all too clever few.

2. Infrastructure means a lot more than marinas and scenic railways. It's Heilbroner's idea of "capital whose value lies in its use to create more capital." Listen to how the New Deal's David Lillienthal talked about infrastructure in stumping for TVA in the forties.

> "Today it is builders and technicians we turn to, men armed not with the axe, rifle, and bowie knife, but with the Diesel

engine, the bulldozer, the giant electric shovel, the retort—and most of all, with an emerging kind of skill, a modern knack of organization and execution. When these men have imagination and faith, they can move mountains; out of their skills, they can create new jobs, relieve human drudgery, give new life and fruitfulness to worn-out lands, put yokes upon the streams, and transmute the minerals of the earth and plants of the field into machines of wizardry to spin out the stuff of a way of life new to this world."

From *Righteous Pilgrim*, by T.H. Watkins, a biography of another eloquent New Dealer, Roosevelt's Secretary of Interior Harold L. Ickes.

I may shudder at images of black topping the forests and "yokes upon the streams."

But I still want to know about the yield implicit in the project, the contribution of infrastructure investment to improved productivity and higher standards of living. Because, "nothing is as important for our economic welfare as productivity growth," writes Economist William J. Baumol in *Productivity and American Leadership, the Long View.* "In an economy whose productivity is growing an increase in outlays on social services can be paid for entirely out of the increment that productivity contributes."

3. We should rebuild the infrastructure with tax-free munis, because they save our states and local governments money when they go to borrow in the "low-cost," tax-free bond market. "Low-cost" is the operative term. The economics for tax exemption are a joke when munis pay practically the same or even more than comparable taxable bonds, without even taking the value of tax exemption into account. And that's the case right now, caused by state and local budget woes, the demise of municipal bond insurance, and hedge funds unwinding their leverage and dumping their munis to meet margin calls. You'll know the municipal bond market is back in shape to do its job of digging roads and laying sewers—and saving the states money in borrowing costs—when the unwinding's done and the tax-free-to-taxable-yield ratio has returned to normal.

4. One other warning, and you read about it here first. Just the threat of taxation cudgeled confessions by almost 100 perps trying to cheat the IRS with yield burning. They sent guys to jail in World War II for cutting corners. There was even a play about it in revival on Broadway: *All My Sons*. No cheating, fellas. It's not allowed in wartime. And we're in a war.

5. A parting shot to our great American cities and states. You're in a hole. I know you can borrow your way out and finance a deficit with good, old GO municipal bonds. And you probably will. But please. *Please* hold back on some of your limited borrowing capacity. Save your seed corn to plant in the infrastructure and grow still more seed corn.

Unless I have the broker's Obligation of Disclosure wrong, consider yourself informed about investing in municipal bonds. I've told you everything I can about munis without knowing more about you or where interest rates are headed. If you're still in a quandary about investing, stop spinning your wheels. Pull yourself together and decide, "Yes …" or "No!"

Photography by Lester Lefkowitz

There's a little bit of cathedral in everything we build.

Epilogue

Build America Bonds Go To War

A DIFFERENT KIND of war bond is fighting a different kind of war than the one we fought with Liberty Bonds and War Bonds in World Wars I and II. They're "Build America Bonds," a new taxable municipal bond, created by the American Recovery and Reinvestment Act to fight the greatest recession since the Great Depression and keep it from turning into a Great Depression II. ARRA gives our states in 2009 and 2010 the option of financing any infrastructure project that qualifies for exemption from federal income taxes with either traditional tax frees or with taxable Build America Bonds ("BABs"). Not since the same kind of war effort in the depths of the Depression, could investment in infrastructure be sitting this pretty.

Why would municipalities go out of their way to borrow at taxable interest rates, when they can borrow tax free? Because Uncle Sam will pick up the tab for 35% of the cost of borrowing, if issuers elect to finance their infrastructure projects with taxable BABs. Between the federal government's 35% and the issuer on the hook for only 65%, municipalities can actually save money and come out ahead borrowing for public works in the taxable bond market. Fine! As a big believer in our cities and states borrowing for capital improvements at the lowest possible interest rate, I am all for Build America Bonds, with one hesitation. When two parties are willing to foot a bill, it is easy for the two of them combined to end up overpaying to dig the tunnel or build the bridge. Indeed, in the first days of the Build America Bond program, California, the New Jersey Turnpike, and New York's Metropolitan Transportation Authority came to market with BABs paying 7.55 percent, 7.33 percent, and 7.40 percent respectively—rates exceeding 30-year Treasuries by at least 350 basis points.

The managers of any new financial instrument price it to come out of the gate at a bang. On top of which, the Build America Bonds were making their debut in a financial crisis, reflecting frenzied credit markets, the plight of the less than triple-A borrower, and the stimulus mentality. Whatever it takes to create jobs and get the economy up and running again goes, price no object.

With it all, the one financial tool we have for building the infrastructure—the municipal bond, albeit taxable municipal bond— has found a mother lode in the deep pockets of a new market: the tax exempt pension and endowment funds. Tax exempt institutions get no additional benefit from owning tax exempt municipal bonds. The trillions they hold in taxable securities are already exempt. So the full return from those 7.55 percent, 7.33 percent, and 7.40 percent taxable BABs goes right to the pension and endowment's bottom line. To oblige, California, which planned on issuing $3 billion BABs, upped its sale and blew out $5 billion. The New Jersey Turnpike likewise upped its sale from $650 million to $1.38 billion. And the MTA from $200 million to $750 million. Those particular BABs may be used only for capital improvements. By law. No refundings. No "working" capital. No deficit financing.

The action, up to this moment of writing, has been in "Direct Pay" Build America Bonds, where the federal subsidy goes directly to the issuer and a tax exempt investor gets to keep the full return. Soon, coming next to a broker near you, is another kind of BAB, "Tax Credit" BABs, where the federal subsidy goes to the investor in the form of a tax credit for 35% of the interest paid by the issuer. As an individual investor in Tax Credit BABs for your personal account, you would end up paying tax on the other 65% at whatever your own personal income tax rate. In your Individual Retirement Account, the full coupon would be tax deferred, and, of course, in your personal account, free of state and local income taxes to local taxpayers in the state where issued.

Ever since Mrs. Anna Thomson Dodge, the automobile heiress, began driving the IRS crazy, clipping tax free municipal bond coupons to the tune of an estimated $40,000 a day and getting away Scot free at tax time, the idea of weaning the states off tax exemption with a taxable bond option has been kicking around. And getting nowhere. States and local governments were doing just fine coming to market at tax free rates in the 80% range of comparable Treasuries. Who needed a taxable bond option? Only the IRS.

I was never a fan of the taxable bond option. But with tax free municipal bonds coming to market at 100% of Treasuries these last couple of years, and the economy in dire shape, I've done an about face. The taxable bond option is simply an idea whose time has come. It's good for issuers, good for investors, and good even for traditional tax free munis. The more tax frees that are replaced by BABs, the lower the cost of borrowing for the tax free munis that still do come to market, and the more stable the resale value of the tax frees you already own.

As someone, who once pasted 25-cent War Stamps in a book and when the book got to $18.75 turned it in for a $25 War Bond due in ten years (all of a 2.87% yield to maturity), I'd like to see Build America Bonds come in affordable denominations for the average working man and working woman, some of whom may even end up tracing their job one day to your investing your savings in a Build America Bond. So, skipping the no-sell tone I professed in the subtitle, *Straight Talk About Tax Free Municipal Bonds For The Troubled Investor Deciding, "Yes…" or "No!"* I ask you, any bonds today?

It's the same thing Irving Berlin asked in 1942 when he wrote and launched the National Defense Savings Bond Campaign and Bugs Bunny sang:

Any Bonds Today?

The tall man with the high hat and the whiskers on his chin
Will soon be knocking at your door and you ought to be in.

The tall man with the high hat will be coming down your way.

Get your savings out when you hear him shout, "Any bonds, today?"

It worked for guns and bombs once. We won the war, didn't we? Here's to making it work again for subways and sewers, bridges and tunnels, the nuts and bolts that underpin our quality of life.

God bless America!

The Entertaining and Highly Informative
Lebenthal Glossary

Accretion
Accrete is what a zero coupon bond does when, instead of spinning off interest from a coupon, it plows the interest back into the bond every six months so that interest can earn interest, build and rebuild on itself, until one day that zero coupon bond has grown in value—accreted—and becomes redeemable at par.

Accrued Interest
It's like buying a house and paying for whatever oil is left in the tank. An adjustment on your confirmation for that portion of the next interest payment that is due to the previous owner. You shell out for accrued interest when you buy a bond. You receive the accrued interest when you sell it.

Additional Bonds Test
The level at which the earnings of a project built by bonds must cover debt service before additional bonds can be floated.

Advance Refunding
The refunding now of a bond even though it is not yet callable. To do that, an issuer floats new bonds and sequesters the money in U.S. government securities to pay off the old debt when it does become callable. The old bonds, having been advance refunded and taken off the books of the issuer, usually step up to triple-A.

Alternative Minimum Tax
Are you a big giver? Do you have substantial deductions for charitable giving, incentive stock options, state and local taxes, and capital gains that

are treated preferentially at tax time? Individuals with the kind of shelters and write-offs the government calls "preferences"—and that includes the interest from so-called private activity bonds—have to compute their taxes two ways: the regular way, taking all the allowed deductions and exclusions, and the Alternative Minimum Tax method, adding the deductions and exclusions minus a $69,950 gimme for couples and $46,200 for singles ($34,975 for marrieds filing separately). The taxpayer will end up owing whichever is greater: the regular 15 percent, 25 percent, 31 percent, 35 percent tax rate on the first calculation; or 26 percent of the AMT add-back calculation (minus the aforementioned gimme) on the first $175,000 ($75,000 for marrieds filing separately) and 28 percent above that.

Amortization of Premium

Let's say you bought a bond at a 110, and it paid off at 100 at maturity. Where'd the premium go? Why, you got it back bit by bit every six months in the coupon, part of which was real interest being earned and part of which was return of principal. In BondSpeak, it's called amortizing the premium. It's actually skimming your own money that you laid out for the premium back into your own pocket.

AON (All Or None)

It means, if we offer a $125,000 block of bonds, you have to buy the whole block—all or none.

APPRECIATION OF DISCOUNT (ALSO CALLED ACCRETION)

The flipside of amortization of premium. It's the steady growth in a discount bond as it slouches toward maturity to reach its full face value.

Arbitrage

In munis, positive arbitrage would occur when an issuer borrows in the low-cost, tax-free bond market, turns around, and invests bond proceeds in higher-yielding taxable Treasuries, and tries to pocket the change. Our strapped municipalities would do it all day long, were it not for the 1986 Tax Reform Act requiring issuers to rebate positive arbitrage earnings to the IRS or lose the exemption on its municipal bonds.

Ask

Ask is the price we charge when we sell you a bond, as opposed to bid, the price we would pay when we buy a bond from you.

Authority

A public body created by a state or municipality to provide for water, housing, transportation, or other community needs and authorized by the legislature to borrow in the tax-free bond market to build the necessary facilities. The name of the state or municipality may be part of the title of the bond. But authorities usually do not have the power to tax. So their bonds are generally secured solely by revenues and charges to the public for using the facility.

Barbell

A strategy for diversifying maturity dates between a bunch of short bonds coming due in two, three, four, five years (for their liquidity) and a bunch of long bonds maturing down the road (for their superior yield), leaving the middle range of maturities empty.

Basis Point

Even though a basis point is 1/100th of a percent—for instance, the difference between a bond yielding 5.99 percent and 6.00 percent—professional bond traders dealing in the millions will kill for one or two of those basis points.

Bearer Bond

In the old days, when municipal bonds came in coupon, no-name, form made "payable to bearer," anyone could cash in their coupons and the bond itself at the end, no questions asked. In 1983, new issues in bearer form were outlawed. Even though a few are still floating around, don't kid yourself. All redemptions are reported to the IRS on form 1099B.

Bid

An offer to buy a bond at a stated price. It's the price you would get selling your bonds to us. For the price we'd turn right around and offer to sell that bond to someone else, look up Ask.

Bond Bank

Sometimes, instead of selling its bonds directly to the public, a small, obscure municipality will borrow from a state bond bank. The bond bank will then issue its own better-known bonds and pay debt service from the pool of interest and principal the bond bank is collecting from the participating localities.

Bond Buyer Index

There's the 20-Bond Index, the 11-Bond Index, and the 25-Bond Revenue Bond Index, all published by the *Bond Buyer*, the municipal bond industry's trade paper. Each index is an average of the yields to maturity of representative municipal bonds and purports to answer the burning question, where's the market?

Bond Fund

A pool of bonds for pools of people of similar investment objectives, offering the flow-through of tax-free income, diversification, reinvestment of dividends, and professional management of your investment in the tax-free bond market. Viz. a mutual fund of municipal bonds.

Bond Indenture

The issuer's covenant with the bondholder setting forth all rights of the bondholder and all obligations of the issuer.

Book Entry

Book entry, you know, just like your money market account, your mutual fund shares, and U.S. T-bills. When you buy a book-entry municipal bond, there is no physical delivery, because there is nothing to deliver. No certificate. No bond to stick in your vault or take out when you decide to sell. Purchases, sales, transfers, even the pledging of bonds as collateral, are simply made via computerized book entry without the redundancy of the bond certificate traveling back and forth in the mail.

Broker

Please, not broker. Nobody's called a broker anymore. At Lebenthal, your personal account executive is your connection to the municipal bond market and the world of finance, and an all-around good egg.

Call, Call Date, Call Price, Call Risk

What an issuer does when it exercises its right to redeem a bond prior to maturity, pay you off, and bump you out of the picture. The terms of the call provision, such as call date, call price, or the circumstances under which bonds may be called, are spelled out up front and in full in the Official Statement.

Certificate of Participation

Instead of issuing bonds for a new municipal facility, the municipality commissions an entity to build the building and lease it back to the town. The entity lays off its right to the rental payments on third parties, namely investors in certificates of participation (COP). The rent flows through to them as COP interest. COP interest is tax free, just like ordinary municipal bond interest. Except for one thing. The revenue source for that interest, the municipality's lease obligation, must be reappropriated every year in the municipality's annual budget.

Clip Coupons

BondSpeak from the old days when municipal bonds came with coupons attached—like tiny, postdated, interest checks, payable to bearer, to be clipped on each interest payment date and deposited in your bank for collection.

Closed-End Fund

This is a mutual fund that sells a fixed number of shares and does not add to the pot whenever new shareholders want in and does not buy back shares as shareholders want out. Instead, shares are traded on an exchange in the so-called "auction process," where the price people are willing to buy and sell at determines the market—not the asset value of the underlying securities.

Coupon Rate

Coupon rate tells you the interest a bond is paying right along. Coupon and coupon rate are still used for the bond's nominal interest rate.

Coverage

The number of times by which the earnings of the project cover what's needed to pay interest and principal on an associated revenue bond.

Credit Risk

The relative assuredness of receiving your interest right along and getting back face value at the end.

Current Coupon

An interest rate on a new issue or old issue fetching a price pretty close to par.

Current Yield

Current yield is how much you are earning here and now and every time you clip a coupon. It does not tell the whole story of how hard your money is working, because it does not take into account any appreciation of discount or amortization of premium at maturity.

CUSIP Number

Every coupon rate and every maturity date of every municipal bond has its own distinctive fingerprint—a nine-digit identification number assigned to it by the Committee on Uniform Securities Identification Procedures (CUSIP).

Dated Date

The official issue date, when interest on a new issue begins accruing.

De Minimis Market Discount Tax

Why glossaries are boring: because they can't explain everything and shouldn't try. Market discount is the discount that comes from a falling bond market rather than an original issue discount that comes from the issuer. The gain on an original issue discount is tax free. The gain on a market discount is subject to tax: capital gains tax, if it doesn't exceed a certain amount. Ordinary income tax, if it does. And that certain amount is the de minimis amount.

De Minimis Rule

Basically, if the discount from issue price at the time of purchase was greater than $2.50 for each full year between the date you paid for the bond and its maturity date, the market discount will be taxed as ordinary income. For more on how this impacts your investment in market discount bonds, call us. 1-800-425-6006.

Dealer

Dealers, as opposed to brokers, act as principals. For a moment in time, we dealers own the bonds we offer for sale, even if we have to buy them from somebody else and turn right around and sell them to you. We make our money on the spread between bid and ask.

Debt Ratio

The ratio of a municipality's debt to its tax base, population, per capita incomes. A measure of ability to pay. Low is good.

Debt Service

The dollar amount of annual interest and principal due on outstanding bonds—this year, next year, and, we always like to know, in the year of maximum annual debt service due.

Debt Service Reserve Fund

A kitty that can be funded from bond proceeds or from tax collections or other revenues that the bond indenture requires to be maintained at a certain level—often an amount equal to one year's maximum annual future debt service.

Default

Like surrender in war, nonpayment of debt service in municipal bonds is unspeakable. A tabulation by Fitch IBCA reports that by March 1999, general purpose tax-supported debt issued between 1979 and 1986 had a cumulative default rate of only 26/100ths of 1 percent. This table comparing muni defaults to corporate defaults was submitted in evidence to a congressional committee holding hearings on a bill to require the rating agencies to base their ratings on the likelihood of default. The bill, the Municipal Bond Fairness Act (HR 6308), got nowhere. But here is its legacy: the default rate for municipal bonds is lower than that of identically rated corporate bonds.

Cumulative Historic Default Rates (in percent)				
Rating Categories	Moody's		S & P	
	Muni	Corp	Muni	Corp
Aaa/AAA	0.00	0.52	0.00	0.60
Aa/AA	0.06	0.52	0.00	1.50
A/A	0.03	1.29	0.23	2.91
Baa/BBB	0.13	4.64	0.32	10.29
Ba/BB	2.65	19.12	1.74	29.93
B/B	11.86	43.34	8.48	53.72
Caa-C/CCC-C	16.58	69.18	44.81	69.19
Investment Grade	0.07	2.09	0.20	4.14
Non-Investment Grade	4.29	31.37	7.37	42.35
All	0.10	9.70	0.29	12.98

Derivative

A financial contract used for hedging, leveraging, and managing risk by taking a position in an asset without having to invest dollar for dollar in the actual asset. Success or failure depends on how closely the derivative tracks the reference asset and is magnified in direct proportion to the leverage involved: the cost of the contract relative to the amount of the asset the contract is for.

Discount

A bond sells for less than the amount you'll get back at maturity because it was either issued at an original issue discount or has fallen in price in the secondary market. Part of the investment return from a discount bond is coupon interest. Part is the gain from cashing in at full face value at maturity.

Dollar Bond

A bond that trades so frequently it is handier to quote it in dollars and cents, like meat and potatoes, than by its yield to maturity.

DTC

The Depository Trust Company in New York City, an industry-owned cooperative, is the world's largest custodian of corporate and municipal securities. DTC holds in its vaults one jumbo security for the whole issue or for each maturity. We sell you a piece of the issue. We send you a confirmation. We record the transaction on our books, and ownership is transferred via book entry from our account at DTC to a separate Lebenthal customer account at DTC. On an interest or principal payment date, DTC credits Lebenthal, and we in turn credit your Lebenthal account.

Duration

A term that is totally removed from people's experience but very useful, like "light-years" to measure distance to the stars or "10!" to quantify pulchritude. Duration weighs the price volatility of a municipal bond, and the greater the duration, the greater the volatility. If duration is one way to express the relative vulnerability of your portfolio to market risk, then duration is a good thing to know (even though there may not be two fellows in the bond business who can tell you how to set your clock by it).

ETF

"E" for exchange, "T" for traded, "F" for fund. An exchange traded fund is not a mutual fund at all, but a stock, traded on exchanges at the net asset value of the securities in the portfolio, subject to the customary brokerage commission. When the portfolio consists of tax-free municipal bonds, that ETF amounts to nothing less than tax-free dividends from a common stock.

Escrow to Maturity
Sequestering the funds now—locking them up with a trustee for the sole purpose of redeeming a bond issue way down the road at maturity, as opposed to its call date. Any existing features for calling in bonds and redeeming them prior to maturity may still rule.

FINRA
Stands for the Financial Industry Regulatory Authority, merged from the NASD and New York Stock Exchange's enforcement arm. FINRA, as enforcer of the Municipal Securities Rulemaking Board's (MSRB's) rules, is responsible for oversight and regulation of all securities firms dealing with the public, including licensing, training, registration, arbitrations, compliance, and fair dealing.

Flat Tax
A flat tax, consumption tax, value added tax—any alternative to the existing income tax system—that would tax the income you spend but not the income you don't spend. If such a flat tax came to pass, municipal bonds would still be tax free, but they would no longer be the only tax-free investment in town.

Flow of Funds
Where the bondholder stands in line with respect to other claims on tolls, fares, and nickels in the meter pledged for debt service.

Full Coupon
Any coupon rate high enough for a bond of a given maturity to sell at par or premium.

Full Faith and Credit General Obligation
This is as close to the absolute as you can get on paper. This is the ultimate pledge of using all the issuer's resources—and taxing power—

to make good and pay you back. Heaven help a municipality that hands out such a pledge lightly.

Gross Revenues
All the revenues, everything in the issuer's cash register. Take the issuer of a hospital bond, for example. Gross revenues would include patient and third-party payments, income from investments, concessions, rentals, unencumbered gifts, grants, donations, etc. Gross revenues are the starting point from which the payment of operations, maintenance, and debt service will then be prioritized and meted out.

Guaranteed
When a revenue bond is also backed by the unqualified taxing power of a state or local government, or when one political entity stands behind the bonds of another with its full faith and credit and taxing power, then, and only then, is the word "guaranteed" used.

Investment Grade
Bonds that are rated in the top four ratings as follows:

Fitch IBCA	Moody's	Standard & Poor's
AAA, AA, A, BBB	Aaa, Aa, A, Baa	AAA, AA, A, BBB

Ladder
A strategy for staggering maturities sequentially (like ladder rungs), so you have bonds coming due and money coming in—to live on, spend, reinvest—commencing in X number of years and regularly thereafter.

Letter of Credit
A form of credit enhancement in which a bank or other financial institution guarantees payment of debt service that is limited to the expiration date of the L.O.C., usually five or so years. If the L.O.C. is not renewed by the institution or one of comparable rating, the bonds must be called.

Leveraging

Augmenting an investment with borrowed funds to goose return by an amount hopefully greater than the cost of the ante. Hint: don't try to leverage by buying municipal bonds on margin. The cost of borrowing to buy or carry tax-free municipal bonds is not deductible.

Liquidity

Turning a security into cash with minimal loss. Put $1 in. Take $1 out when you need it. Now that's liquidity.

Mandatory Call

The circumstances—unexpended bond proceeds, mortgage prepayments, insurance reimbursement, declaration of taxability—under which a bond must be called by the issuer. Not may, must.

Market Discount

When the price you pay for a bond is less than the original issue price, and the discount comes from a falling bond market. The gain at maturity or on sale for a market discount is treated one way by the IRS and another way for an original issue discount that comes from the issuer (in which case, it isn't taxed at all).

Market Risk

The vulnerability of any fixed-income investment to changing interest rates in the economy and possible loss in value if sold before maturity.

Marketability

Liquidity is getting out what you put in. Marketability is the availability of ready buyers, the ease of selling your bond—if, as, and when you want your money—depending always on its current market value.

Markup

The amount of spread between bid and ask. In other words, between what a dealer pays for the bond and what he or she offers to sell it at.

MSRB

The Municipal Securities Rulemaking Board, the body that writes the rules for regulating the underwriting, buying, and selling of all municipal bonds.

Muni

The short, friendly handle for the municipal bonds of our great American states and their counties, cities, towns, and political subdivisions and authorities—and Puerto Rico, as well. As a commonwealth, the interest income from Puerto Rico munis is tax free federally as well as in all states of the Union. The same holds true for Guam and any other commonwealth, territory, or possession of the United States.

Municipal Bond

A municipal bond is evidence of the collective debt of a community. It is a promise to pay a fixed sum of money on a definite date in the future at a fixed rate of interest. It shows that some municipality needed money for the public good. You can't get up in the morning, take a shower, a subway, a bus, go under the river, or over the bridge without a municipal bond touching your life. And the interest is tax free, federally, and free of state and local taxes in most states of the Union where the bond was issued.

Municipal Bond Insurance

An insurance policy guaranteeing payment of municipal bonds. The insurer's obligation to pay principal and interest on defaulted bonds in full and on time is non-cancelable, unlimited, and unconditional. Even without the third-party endorsement of triple-A ratings, the insurance could prove of practical value in an economic downturn.

Municipal Notes

Notes are short-term borrowings for a year or less to tide a municipality over during gaps in cash flow. They are issued in anticipation of taxes to be collected (TANS), revenues to be received (RANS), or from the proceeds of a long-term bond sale to be held later on (BANS).

Net Revenues

Revenues actually available for debt service after payments, such as operations and maintenance, that might come first, spelled out in the Flow of Funds.

Odd Lot

Could be a block of bonds under $25,000, $100,000, $1,000,000. Depends on the house you're dealing with.

Official Statement

The indenture is the bondholder's contract with the issuer, setting forth the terms of the deal. And its key provisions are also found in the Official Statement, an abundant disclosure document we are required by securities law to send you when you buy a new issue in the primary market. What there really ought to be is a law making sure you read it.

Open-End Fund

An investment company that is constantly selling shares and adding to portfolio as new money comes in and redeeming shares as money goes out. If actively managed, it doesn't just sit there waiting for bonds in the portfolio to mature, but buys, sells, holds, and trades in an attempt to fulfill the fund's objective.

Optional Call

The right of an issuer to redeem bonds at a certain date and at a certain price before maturity. Other call features may exist, but the optional call is the one that must appear on your confirmation.

Original Issue Discount

Although individuals may go for juicy coupon rates at par, one or two or more maturities in a new issue may come with lower coupon rates at discounts. (To give institutional investors and some individuals the potential for capital gains.) The accretion of original issue discount is considered a part of total return coming from the issuer and, as such, is tax free. The gain from any market appreciation on top of normal accretion is subject to the applicable tax.

Overlapping Debt

Debt burden is not just your municipality's own bonds but the bonds of your school district, your county, and any other overlapping jurisdiction that local taxpayers are responsible for.

Par Call

The scheduled date a bond becomes callable at par with no premium for bumping you out of the picture early.

Par Value

The face value of a bond at maturity: 100 percent!

Performance

It can be good or bad. Performance is the bond trader's success or failure at making money in the bond market, buying, selling, and trading opportunistically.

Premium

A bond whose price is above par. All it means is that a bond quoted to you at 105 is selling at 105 percent of par, or $1,050 for each $1,000 of face value.

Premium Call

This is really throwing you a bone. The first optional call date is often at a premium, to compensate you for having to give up a bond with a big, beautiful interest rate.

Pre-Re

Shorthand for a bond that has been advanced or pre-refunded.

Pre-Sale Order Taking Period

A one- or two-day period during which retail investors, like you, as opposed to big financial institutions, have first crack at a new issue. Still doesn't leave much time to noodle on it.

Price to Par Call

Callable bonds must be quoted and offered at the "worse." The "worse" is the lesser of yield to maturity, yield to the premium call, or yield to the par call. If by some stroke of luck the bonds do remain uncalled and do go out to maturity, the investor would wind up with a higher return. Gravy. Found money!

Prior Lien

This dictates who has first claim on the issuer's resources. You, the bondholder? Or someone else?

Public Offering Price

The price at which a new issue of bonds is initially offered by all members of the underwriting syndicate for a set period of time. If you're worried, "Am I paying the right price?" it's a comfort knowing the public offering price is the same price to one and all. For the shares of a mutual fund or units of a unit investment trust, the public offering price is the price at which the shares must be priced and sold, usually based on the net asset value (NAV) of the underlying securities, determined at arm's length by a third party pricing service.

RAN, TAN, TRAN, BAN

Revenue Anticipation Notes. Tax Anticipation Notes, Tax and Revenue Anticipation Notes, Bond Anticipation Notes. Short-term municipal borrowings of one year or less. See Municipal Notes.

Ratings

Rating agencies grade the creditworthiness of municipal bonds. Numbers go in, but there is no single formula by which the AAAs, AAs, As, and BBBs come out. Excellence can still be present in a lesser-rated bond, even if to a lesser degree. The upper four ratings are generally considered investment grade, adequate security for investors seeking the basic assuredness of interest and safety of principal that attracts one to municipals in the first place.

Rating Definitions (Moody's)

Aaa

Issuers or issues rated Aaa demonstrate the strongest creditworthiness relative to other US municipal or tax-exempt issuers or issues.

Aa

Issuers or issues rated Aa demonstrate very strong creditworthiness relative to other US municipal or tax-exempt issuers or issues.

A

Issuers or issues rated A present above average creditworthiness relative to other US municipal or tax-exempt issuers or issues.

Baa

Issuers or issues rated Baa represent average creditworthiness relative to other US municipal or tax-exempt issuers or issues.

Ba

Issuers or issues rated Ba demonstrate below average creditworthiness relative to other US municipal or tax-exempt issuers or issues.

B

Issuers or issues rated B demonstrate weak creditworthiness relative to other US municipal or tax-exempt issuers or issues.

Caa

Issuers or issues rated Caa demonstrate very weak creditworthiness relative to other US municipal or tax-exempt issuers or issues.

Ca

Issuers or issues rated Ca demonstrate extremely weak creditworthiness relative to other US municipal or tax-exempt issuers or issues.

C

Issuers or issues rated C demonstrate the weakest creditworthiness relative to other US municipal or tax-exempt issuers or issues.

NOTE: Moody's appends numerical modifiers 1, 2, and 3 to each generic rating category from Aa through Caa. The modifier 1 indicates that the issuer or obligation ranks in the higher end of its general rating category; the modifier 2 indicates a mid-range ranking; and the modifier 3 indicates a ranking in the lower end of that generic rating category.

Source: Moody's Investor Service, Global Credit Research

Real Rate of Return

The "take-home pay" from an investment after taxes and inflation. Tax-free municipal bonds at least eliminate income taxes from the equation.

Retail Market

Not the banks, not insurance companies, not mutual funds or big financial institutions, but you, the individual retail investor, are the mainstay of the municipal bond market. Individuals own 71 percent of the munis outstanding, either directly or indirectly through mutual funds.

Revenue Bond

These are bonds secured by tolls, rentals, mortgage payments, tuitions, fees, or charges to the user instead of taxes. Among the projects financed by revenue bonds are transportation systems, turnpikes, hospitals, public housing, stadiums, airports, colleges, water and sewer systems, solid waste and resource recovery systems—in fact any municipal enterprise that sustains itself by selling its service to the public.

Risk

The exposure to loss arising from market volatility, changing interest rates, headlines, legislative threats to tax exemption, changing fortunes of the issuer, and the unpredictable outcome of markets driven by psychology as well as fundamentals.

Round Lot

A round lot is a block of bonds with a face value of $25M, $100M, $500M, or more, depending where you shop.

Secondary Market

The resale market that comes into being when the initial purchasers of a new issue begin trading their bonds.

Securitization

The bundling and turning of a pool of illiquid assets into marketable securities, whose shareholders then participate proportionately in the cash flows from, say, mortgages, car loans, credit card debt, even back taxes and derivatives, and the losses and gains therefrom.

Senior Lien

A bond with first dibs on revenues earmarked for debt service.

Serial Bond

To avoid having to pay off an entire issue in a lump sum in a single year, a municipality will often retire its debt in annual installments over the anticipated life of the project by issuing its bonds serially, so they mature in staggered years.

Settlement Date

You buy a bond today (trade date). Three business days later is the settlement date, and your payment is due.

SIFMA

Stands for Securities Industry and Financial Markets Association, the trade organization of banks, brokers, dealers who underwrite and sell municipal, U.S. government, mortgage-backed, corporate, and federal agency bonds.

Sinker

A call feature—or the kitty into which the funds are set aside periodically—to redeem part or all of an issue before maturity, as revenues come in and are available to do so.

Spread

The difference between bid/ask, wholesale/retail—reflecting the markup or intended profit in a bond.

Tax Bracket

Under our government's progressive tax system, when income brackets increase, the tax rate in that bracket increases, from 15 percent to 25 percent ... 33 percent ... 35 percent. If a taxable investment bumps you into the next higher tax bracket, that's the bracket to use in computing the tax savings from switching to tax-free municipal bonds.

Tax Deferred

As applied to a tax-deferred retirement account, this means no tax on gains, growth, or income are due right now. You will be taxed when you take your money out.

Tax Free

Careful how you use the word, because tax free applies solely to freedom from federal *income* tax and from state and local *income* taxes to residents of the state where the bond was issued. Estate taxes, capital gains taxes, the alternative minimum tax, and the Social Security tax computation (requiring retirees to include tax-free municipal bond interest in determining taxes due on Social Security benefits) all apply, even to tax-free municipal bonds.

Tax-Free-to-Taxable-Yield-Ratio

Always remember, a dollar from a tax-free municipal bond that's yours to keep is worth more than a taxable dollar. The tax-free-to-taxable-yield expresses the muni yield as a percentage of any taxable alternative you care to compare to the muni.

Tax Reform Act of 1986

The law largely governing the issuance of tax-free municipal bonds today. It prohibits the issuance of tax exempts for certain nongovernmental purposes outright. It allows certain other nongovernmental bonds to be issued subject to volume caps. It limits the types of bonds banks can buy and still take the deduction for their cost of carry. It limits how many times a bond can be refunded and still qualify for tax exemption. It requires municipal issuers to rebate to Uncle Sam positive arbitrage earned on bond proceeds temporarily invested in construction funds and debt reserve funds. It created the alternative minimum tax on certain private activity bonds.

Tax Swapping

You sell your depressed bonds. You buy someone else's (not substantially identical, please). And in the exchange, you realize an actual loss to use against gains or income. You not only save money in taxes, but you wind up with bonds replacing yours.

T+3

This is a securities industry requirement that we pay you and you pay us within three business days following a trade. (T stands for trade date; 3 stands for days.)

Taxable Equivalent

The amount that a bank or other taxable alternative would have to pay you before taxes so that after the taxes in your income bracket, the net at least equals the tax-free return of a municipal bond you are considering. In determining if tax exempts are suitable for you, the idea isn't for the municipal bond to just match the take-home from a taxable alternative but to top it.

Taxable Municipal Bonds

The 1986 Tax Act that governs the issuance of tax-free municipal bonds today bans tax-free municipal bonds for certain purposes deemed nongovernmental. Issuers are perfectly free to issue them—but as taxable municipal bonds. The existence of municipal bonds that are taxable opens the market for munis to whole new buyers: tax deferred retirement accounts and tax-exempt organizations, whose investments are already tax deferred or tax exempt and don't particularly benefit from tax-free munis. Taxable munis are usually free of state and local taxes to residents of the state where issued.

Total Return

All cash flow from interest and dividends plus compounding of reinvestment plus any gains or minus any losses. Total return does not include commissions, getting in and getting out costs, and taxes.

Trade Date

It's the date the transaction is executed. Use trade date, not settlement date, to determine whether a gain or loss is long term or short term.

Unit Investment Trust

A municipal bond U.I.T. is an unmanaged, closed-end portfolio of municipal bonds that have been assembled by an investment company to provide unit holders with a steady, tax-free return. Once the bonds have been packaged and all the units (representing undivided interests in the underlying trust) have been sold, trading bonds in and out of the portfolio ceases (other than to get rid of any bond that's in trouble and distribute the proceeds to the unit holders).

When Issued

Even though the terms may be set, until the bonds have actually been delivered by the issuer to the underwriter, new issues are offered and confirmed conditionally like this: "when, as, and if issued?"

Yield Curve

It can be positive (the longer the maturity, the greater the return). It can be negative. It can be inverted. It can be humped. It's a graph showing bond returns relative to maturities.

Yield to Maturity

The most important measure of how hard money is working in a bond. Clip those coupons right along. Cash in the bond itself at the end. And you—or your heirs—will receive the promised yield to maturity.

Yield to Call

It's the same idea as yield to maturity, except that yield to call is calculated to the call date and call price (which is not always par, but sometimes a premium).

Zero Coupon Bond

Traditional municipal bonds pay out interest right along. Zero coupon bonds pay out nothing right along. Zero. Goose egg. Zeroes are always issued below face value. Instead of paying out interest in the form of current income to be spent and frittered away, the interest is added to the pot and earns interest. Then that tax-free interest earns even more tax-free interest, building and rebuilding on itself right up to the day of maturity. Down the road, you wind up with a big lump sum. Tax free.

The Index
With More Than One Clue For
Finding What You're Looking For

M

insured ratings, 61-63
triple-A, vi, 6, 7, 29, 32-33, 35-36, 52,
   61-64, 67, 93, 102, 108, 111, 123
weighing against yield, 72-75, 85
Real Rate of Return, 25, 128
   option,
Rendell, Edward G. (governor of Pennsylvania),
   102
Rime of Ancient Mariner, 68
Risk, 4, 10, 31, 40, 49, 65-68, 77-79, 97, 119
Rosetta Stone, metaphor for taxable equivalent
   yield table 11-12

S
Securities and Exchange Commission (SEC)
   auction rate securities, 67
   investigation NYC bond sales, 2-3
   Matthews & Wright case, 45
   plain-english prospectuses, 75
Second Safest Investment in America,
   advertisement, 2-3
Securities Industry and Financial Markets
   Association (SIFMA), 130
Securities Investor Protection Corporation
   (SIPC), 70
Shearson Lehman, 65
Smith, Darwin family of Detroit, 54
South Carolina v. Baker, 65
Sovereigns need to preserve credit, 27, 96
Spread(s) in price
   between bid and ask, 17, 56-57,
      73, 117, 122
   between ratings, 31
Standard & Poor's 1990s default study, 7
State Revolving Funds (SRFs), 35-38,
   100-102
Suitability (who belongs in munis and
   which ones?) 11, 30, 51-57, 59-60
Supreme Court, U.S.,
   S. Carolina v. Baker: constitutional

basis for tax exemption overruled,
x, 10

Faitoute Iron & Steel Co. v. City of
Asbury Park, practical limit on
bondholder rights, 3

Davis v. Kentucky, uphold states
exempting own and taxing out of
state bonds, 14

Supreme Court, Washington,
invalidates WPPSS obligation to pay, 43

T

Take-or-pay contract(s), 42-43

Taxable Equivalent Yield Table,
as Rosetta Stone, 11-12

Tax(es)

alternative minimum tax (AMT), x, 10, 12,
80, 93, 131

capital gains tax, 10, 53, 77, 111, 117

estate tax, 10, 130

flat tax, opposition to, 10-11

market discount, 80, 116-117, 122

nongovernmental bonds, 10, 131

private activity bonds, x, 10, 12, 80, 112, 113

social security benefits, 5, 15, 83, 95, 123

Tax exemption, 9-14, 131

case for, x, 10, 18, 103, 109

defense of, 91-93

retroactive removal of, 45-46

under a flat tax, 10

Tax-free-to-taxable-yield ratio, 18-19, 103, 131

Tax Reform Act, 1986, 44, 112, 131

Tender Option Bonds (TOBs), 32-33, 92

Timing, investment, 17-20, 23-24

Treasury bonds (U.S. Treasuries), 4, 12, 18-19,
28, 63, 108-109, 112

Treasury Inflation Protected Securities (TIPS),
25-26

U

UBS, 68

V

Variety "laying an egg" metaphor for
"29" Crash, 65
Volcker, Paul, 16, 22

W

Wachovia, 68
Washington Public Power Supply System
(WPPSS, "Whoops,") default, ix, 42-43, 65,
68, 96
Wrong doing, ix, 39-50

Y

"Yes ..." or "No!" deciding, xi, 59, 76,104
Yield burning, 47–50
        Lissak, Michael, 46
Yield curve, 21-23
"Yield implicit in the project,"
        productivity gain from infrastructure
        investment, 95-96, 103
Yield to maturity, 15-20, 36-38, 96, 133

Z

Zero coupon bond(s), 53, 111, 133

BUY A SHARE OF THE FUTURE IN YOUR COMMUNITY

These certificates make great holiday, graduation and birthday gifts that can be personalized with the recipient's name. The cost of one S.H.A.R.E. or one square foot is $54.17. The personalized certificate is suitable for framing and will state the number of shares purchased and the amount of each share, as well as the recipient's name. The home that you participate in "building" will last for many years and will continue to grow in value.

Here is a sample SHARE certificate:

YES, I WOULD LIKE TO HELP!

*I support the work that Habitat for Humanity does and I want to be part of the excitement! As a donor, I will receive periodic updates on your construction activities but, more importantly, I know my gift will help a family in our community realize the dream of homeownership. **I would like to SHARE in your efforts against substandard housing in my community!** (Please print below)*

PLEASE SEND ME _____ SHARES at $54.17 EACH = $ $_____

In Honor Of: _____

Occasion: (Circle One)   *HOLIDAY*   *BIRTHDAY*   *ANNIVERSARY*

    OTHER: _____

Address of Recipient: _____

Gift From: _____ *Donor Address:* _____

Donor Email: _____

I AM ENCLOSING A CHECK FOR $ $_____ PAYABLE TO HABITAT FOR HUMANITY <u>OR</u> PLEASE CHARGE MY VISA OR MASTERCARD (*CIRCLE ONE*)

Card Number _____ Expiration Date: _____

Name as it appears on Credit Card _____ Charge Amount $ _____

Signature _____

Billing Address _____

Telephone # Day _____ Eve _____

PLEASE NOTE: Your contribution is tax-deductible to the fullest extent allowed by law.
Habitat for Humanity • P.O. Box 1443 • Newport News, VA 23601 • 757-596-5553
www.HelpHabitatforHumanity.org

LaVergne, TN USA
16 October 2009

161150LV00005B/1/P